the inner
adventure

the
adve

the inner adventure

Conversations

....

**Louis Calaferte &
Jean-Pierre Pauty**

*Translated from the French
by Willard Wood*

THE MARLBORO PRESS/NORTHWESTERN
Northwestern University Press
Evanston, Illinois

Cet ouvrage, publié dans le cadre d'un programme d'aide à la publication, bénéficie du soutien du Ministère des Affaires étrangères et du Service Culturel de l'Ambassade de France aux Etats-Unis. [This work, published as part of a program of aid for publication, received support from the French Ministry of Foreign Affairs and the Cultural Services of the French Embassy in the United States.]

The Marlboro Press/Northwestern
Northwestern University Press
Evanston, Illinois 60208-4210

Originally published in French under the title *L'aventure intérieure.* Copyright © 1994 by Éditions Julliard. English translation copyright © 2003 by Northwestern University Press. Published 2003 by the Marlboro Press/Northwestern. All rights reserved.

Printed in the United States of America
10 9 8 7 6 5 4 3 2 1

ISBN 0-8101-6066-8 (cloth)
ISBN 0-8101-6067-6 (paper)

Library of Congress Cataloging-in-Publication Data
Calaferte, Louis, 1928–
    [Aventure intérieure. English]
    The inner adventure : conversations / Louis Calaferte and Jean-Pierre Pauty ; translated from the French by Willard Wood.
        p. cm.
    Includes bibliographical references.
    ISBN 0-8101-6066-8 (cloth : alk. paper)—ISBN 0-8101-6067-6 (pbk. : alk. paper)
    1. Calaferte, Louis, 1928– —Interviews. 2. Authors, French—20th century—Interviews.
I. Pauty, Jean-Pierre. II. Wood, Willard. III. Title.
PQ2663.A389 Z46213 2001
848'.91409—dc21

                                                                        2001006686

The paper used in this publication meets the minimum requirements of the American National Standard for Information Sciences—Permanence of Paper for Printed Library Materials, ANSI Z39.48-1984.

BOOK DESIGN BY EVELYN C. SHAPIRO

contents

············

the inner adventure

FOR NATHALIE

These interviews were conducted in Paris on July 22 and 23, 1993.

During the winter of 1993 to 1994, Louis Calaferte was taken seriously ill. Concerned about the book's future, he expressed his wish that it be published quickly.

On May 2, 1994, Calaferte died at a clinic in Dijon.

Thanks are due to all those who made it possible for this book to exist in the form Calaferte wanted.

—Jean-Pierre Pauty

**The life of every man
is a path toward himself,
the attempt at a path,
sketches of a track.
None has ever managed
to be entirely himself,
though each attempts
to become himself,
some in obscurity,
others in greater light,
each as he is able.**

—Hermann Hesse

Louis Calaferte at the time of writing *Septentrion*. "When the protagonist in *Septentrion*, who is in fact yourself, undergoes a sort of epiphany in front of Dali's *Christ*...." Mornant, 1958. (Photograph, collection G. Calaferte)

preface

Louis Calaferte was a character out of Pasolini, a *ragazzo di vita* who emerged from the underclass slums of Turin and sought the light in a setting of poverty, violence, sex, and blood.

For any man who feels inwardly split, oscillating between the acceptance of life and the refusal of it, between the meaning of existence and its meaninglessness, the *Carnets* of Louis Calaferte from the very first constitute the most perfect of mirrors, then very rapidly become a staunch lifeline.

That reader will discover a man struggling with himself in realms sunk in shadow, a man seeking dignity of being, a man prey to what Kierkegaard calls the "sickness unto death," despair.

"I am led to anguish by the awareness of human realities."[1]

"I pass through stages that go from implicit acceptance, tinged with mysticism, to morbid negativity."[2]

A photograph of Louis Calaferte taken in 1958 shows him at the time he was writing *Septentrion*. As with the captives in Plato's cave, he seems to have only one way out: upward. Upward, toward that point straight above where he has carefully placed a first symbol, Dali's *Christ*—a painting before which he declares in the last pages of *Septentrion:* "They could bolt their doors, all of them, as many of them as there might be, but I for one saw my place as by the side of that Cross."

In this same photograph we discover, on the horizontal plane, a human skull, the ultimate reminder: memento mori. Seldom has the photograph of a writer at work so well caught what Louis Calaferte himself defined as the opposing forces tearing at him:

1. The symbolism of the Cross: the quartering of the two dimensions of being, horizontal and vertical
2. The symbolism of salvation through knowledge, defying Faustian negation

Faust-Calaferte then asks himself: Will I be allowed to recover the state of innocence?

At the end of *Le Chemin de Sion,* he notes, "The inner adventure has certainly been worth undergoing, but I no longer have the energy to proceed any farther."[3]

Will his "spiritual hunt" run itself out in the desert, as did that of Arthur Rimbaud? At the conclusion of his *Season in Hell,* Rimbaud wrote, "Spiritual combat is as brutal as the battle men wage against men; but the vision of justice is God's pleasure alone."

Will Calaferte hold fast to "the ground gained"? The "hour of death, the hour of flight" seems to sound at the beginning of *L'Or et le Plomb.* The negative forces that threaten to split him are assailing him. Moments of affliction: ". . . the fact is that at the deepest levels of my being suicide is envisioned with the soothing certainty of the inevitable."

After this new descent into hell, Calaferte speaks of a "grave moral crisis." Faith and the desire to live reappear. The foray continues.

Not until several years later (in *Le Spectateur immobile*) does he observe a profound change taking place in himself: "Over the last two or three years my mental universe has grown calmer, clearer; I move over restful terrain."[4]

What we have here is a far cry from a faith known within the comfort of dogmas invented by the churches—dogmas that inevitably rhyme with the will to power and its dictatorial aberrations. For Calaferte, faith is not a theological concept but a wrestling deep within oneself, where each individual must examine his or her conscience. The influence here is of Kierkegaard: "One must preach not in church but in the street; and for that one must be not an orator but a witness: in other words faith, that anxiety, must manifest itself in your life."[5]

Louis Calaferte's literary narratives are likewise marked by the inner adventure: "My literary work is in fact nothing more than a diary in disguise."

Certain simplistic questioners sometimes asked him to be more clear about what they called "irreconcilable" aspects of his work: the pulsions of death, of sex, and of faith in the eternal. The apparent duality within his person, within his work, is in fact no more than the expression of a searching for unity. Those phenomena arising from conflicting energies are phenomena he was perfectly conscious of and of whose secret alchemy he was aware. But it was therein precisely that he would measure the limits of knowledge, measure his own powerlessness: What can you do when obscure forces unleash themselves in man?

"Twofold expression of the One. It takes two directions, one of them being toward sublimation, through which it joins the All; the other does not reach the All, and thereby decomposes.

"Errancy of bewitched souls, nonetheless the product of a Unique Principle."[6]

If a first consequence of this taking into account of the whole of being was censorship and banning (Calaferte's *Septentrion*), it also occasioned a profound misunderstanding that was fueled by those who focused upon only one aspect of his writings— their darkness, their misanthropy, their pornography—without ever alluding to the other side of his mental universe: its spirituality, its mysticism, its celebration of beauty.

As early as the second volume of his *Carnets,* Louis Calaferte notes this incomprehension of his undertaking: "I am dumbfounded at the rudimentary way in which these so-called literary critics do their reading nowadays. For example, *Hinterland* and *Limitrophe* were unmistakably about the initiatory 'journey,' already foreshadowed plainly enough, it seems to me, in *Portrait de l'enfant.*"[7]

Later, when *La Mécanique des femmes* [translated into English as *The Way It Works with Women*] was published, the misunderstanding deepened further. Some judged it to be a work of pornography, while the author described it as one of the stages of initiation: "Eroticism is an initiatory path, not toward possession but toward a sort of discovery of what the other may convey . . . knowledge of what the world might be, of 'the mechanics of the world.' There's the way it works with women . . . there is also the way it works with the world!" (See pages 65–66 and 68.)

Like Søren Kierkegaard, Louis Calaferte designated existence as the sole basis of creativity, of thought, and of knowledge.

Anything not based on experience, on the "experienced true," to Calaferte smacked of dishonesty, of imposture. This is what people found frightening: his experience of human reality, his entomological characterization of himself and others. "Any book that is not a rape of oneself has no cause to exist."

By writing, the writer modifies himself, metamorphoses, lives an undertaking of perpetual regeneration. There is an alchemy between experience and writing.

Once Louis Calaferte was aware of the modification going forward within him, of his spiritual and intellectual rebirth, writing came for him to belong to the realm of the sacred.

Writing *Septentrion,* he clearly saw creating as the expression of the divine. He placed a quotation from the Apostle John at the head of his book: "Set down in a book what you see." And never afterward was he to stray from this principle.

Without question this encounter with the holy, an encounter in which he glimpsed the light, came about only as the result of that difficult internal struggle, that total dislocation of his soul.

The metaphysical experience of Louis Calaferte is among the deepest, among the richest, for being among those that strain most toward the absolute.

—Jean-Pierre Pauty

conversations

The inner-directed man
no longer belongs to any Church:
he may be seen in a sense
to represent a perfected being,
the one that Kierkegaard aspired to:
the Isolate.
If it were the case,
such a slippage would immediately
find its explanation, its raison d'être,
its metaphysical justification. . . .
The tragic actuality
weighing on the world
may need, and very likely will need,
a mind, a will, a faith thus firmly governed.

—Louis Calaferte, *Droit de cité*

. . . .

Louis Calaferte. Blaisy-Bas, 1992. (Photograph, Louis Monier)

break with the past

....

Jean-Pierre Pauty: If you have no objection, we will discuss only those of your books that have appeared in the last few years: *L'Incarnation, Les Sables du temps, Memento mori, Le Spectateur immobile, La Mécanique des femmes* [*The Way It Works with Women*], *Droit de cité, C'est la guerre* [*C'est la Guerre*], and, of course, the book you have just finished, *L'Homme vivant.*

As we were taking our places at the table, you said to me that this period of literary creation marked a break with your previous one.

Louis Calaferte: Yes I did. My chronology is a little uncertain, but I think there was a break in time between the publication of *Promenade dans un parc* and *L'Incarnation.* Actually, it was a period of summing up. Several times in the course of my life I have needed to reflect on what I had done, on what I wanted to do, on what I am, and on my literary development, because if there is one thing I cannot put up with in art it is repetitiveness. I believe that once you say a thing, it's said. Someone else may come back to it, but you can't. For me, *L'Incarnation* signals a new approach toward the descriptive, which presents a serious problem in literature. Theoretically, and even practically, you can't do without description in a literary work. Yet that is the part that weighs a text down, that dates it, causes it to age, and sometimes makes it hard or uncomfortable to read—or even totally unreadable. Only very recently a little incident revived this concern of mine. Some schoolchildren, adolescents, were having to study Balzac. Unanimously, they showed a kind of hostility, not toward the substance of the text itself but toward its weight of description. We know, of course, how Balzac worked—he was paid by the line, which offers one explanation, but there persists in the French novelistic tradition this need for description, a description that is not internalized. It is a description of externals, something laid on the outside, a decoration, and the decorative is what it is, an ornamenting that most often works against essentialness.

I began taking this direction in *L'Incarnation.* I went on with it in *La Mécanique des femmes, C'est la guerre, L'Homme vivant,* and at the moment I am trying, with considerable difficulty, let me add, to write brief stories where only the emotional essence is conveyed, with the descriptive element being reduced almost to nothing. Which is why writing *L'Incarnation* was, in that sense, a kind of break with the past, a change.

Pauty: André Malraux was among the first to say that the novel's descriptive element died with the arrival of motion pictures, that film would take over this function.

Calaferte: That's correct, in the sense that images, film, television (especially television, for as regards film you have a different problem, there being serious cinema and commercial movies), deal with the anecdotal, behind which are nothing but feelings, sensations, emotions, the primary affections. With television, you are always on the primary level.

Malraux's thinking may have been good, but his execution

wasn't. Sorry, but I have to say Malraux was a poor writer. He lacked the professional conscience every writer ought to have directing his attention to the deep and lasting dynamism represented in the sentence—and in the composition of the sentence.

Someone else I am much closer to, though with reservations this time that are not of a literary nature, is Céline. It was Céline who said, "Either writing will become telegraphic or there will be no more writing." I believe this is true. Given the context of speed, of the need for rapid absorption. Don't forget, our society is undergoing not only a social mutation but an intellectual one as well. Today all the young people go to school and at whatever level they emerge it is with a capacity to understand, with knowledge. From there on, the decorative is going to appear superfluous. You are obliged to distrust it as there is nothing behind it but insincerity. The decorative is insincerity, fabrication.

Pauty: Søren Kierkegaard believed that the aesthetic could not by itself embrace the whole of truth, all its complexities. According to him, there had to be another level as well.

Calaferte: There you are.

Pauty: Getting back to Céline, don't you think he is somewhat boastful in claiming to have invented a style? When you hear him speak, you hear that same style, that very abrupt, very staccato way of saying things. Aren't a man and his style one and the same?

Calaferte: Yes, yes. I think so. It's the poor writers who invent something. The others go along with their own nature, and their times. There is a level of continuity ranging through thought. I believe that in authentic writers—here I am making no judgment as to value—there exists a desire, begotten of necessity, that causes style to derive effectively from the individual. It is closely bound up with the actual person. Céline is a literary force. Here I am not talking about his grave political errors, his very grave political errors.

Pauty: Looking at his work, don't you feel the worm was in the fruit from the start? Right from *Journey to the End of the Night* he points the finger at everyone in the world except himself. Isn't this the mental approach that leads to finding a scapegoat able to resolve one's own problems, a way of projecting everything onto the "other"—the Jew, the Black, the Arab, in different eras?

Calaferte: I am familiar with this theory, which must be sound, but I think it needs to be nuanced somewhat. We should have a further look at Céline's case, at the shadowy areas in certain artists. You know, they banned my third book, *Septentrion,* on the pretext of pornography. I believed it at the time, that was back in 1963. I have since reread *Septentrion* in part, and when it was republished twenty years after its initial appearance, thanks to Gérard Bourgadier at Editions Denoël, I noticed that the press's hostility toward it had not abated. I have the impression that it was banned more for its anarchistic and libertarian content. That is above all what provoked the powers-that-be and not really the pornography.

Actually, the powers-that-be are never very upset by pornography, this whole business is practically legendary. When they attack Baudelaire, what they find blameworthy isn't so much his pornography, which is practically nonexistent, as his direction in life. This, in the eyes of the State, is far more serious.

Pauty: Yet with your epigraph from the gospel of Saint John at the beginning of *Septentrion* you clearly indicated that your approach was essentially mystical, spiritualistic. Did your censors choose not to notice this? Did they see only the sex?

Calaferte: It's not that they didn't want to notice it, but there is nothing more dangerous than a man with profoundly anarchical views, along with all the religious and intellectual content that may enter his thinking. For the powers-that-be I belong in the category of men who, if not dangerous, are at least to be kept at a distance.

My literary life is evidence of this, and my life as a man as well, these being but one and the same thing to me. On the material plane, my life has been the consequence of the fierce ostracization that has now begun to loosen a little. Or so it seems. . . . So it seems. . . .

Pauty: That is the price a person must pay to preserve the freedom of his critical spirit. He can then be "appropriated" neither by the right nor the left.

Calaferte: It is no longer even a question of political divisions. It goes far beyond that.

Pauty: Yet all the artists who have been "appropriated" by politicians have practiced self-censorship and kept silent to the point of dishonesty regarding the most serious matters.

Calaferte: They weren't anarchists, they were careerists! That's what any man is who allows himself to be appropriated! Let him not complain afterward about having been appropriated.

Pauty: In the beginning, Malraux was a revolutionary, a communist, then he supported the conservatives.

Calaferte: Malraux is one of those very Parisianesque people who while yet young draw up a plan for their so-called literary career—of which not much remains at the end. Malraux is not the only example, there are others just as famous. These are people who have a calculating view of the world, they are very conspicuous social successes. Their thinking hews close to the systems we are familiar with, the democratic ones and those that aren't. All of that means nothing to me.

Today the view of man that I have is entirely religious; more than that: entirely divine. One mustn't let oneself be jarred by my use of the word "religious." I haven't found any other; but in my mind it is in no way connected to the dogma belonging to churches.

I am thinking of a sort of divinization of man, varying in degree but in no way amenable to systematizations, whether political or of any other kind. For the moment, my thinking stands at that point.

Pauty: The democracy you dream of, is this not a myth, the ancient dream of Greek philosophy?

Calaferte: I am doubtless a utopian. But I simply say that for certain individuals there are "possibles." That's all. Just "possibles." At the level of the mass of humanity these "possibles" will be precious. I do not ask for more.

I want to be utopian insofar as utopian ideas are evolutionary ideas. They are never regressive ideas. This must be pointed out.

Pauty: Even if utopianism leads to frustrated hopes?

Calaferte: It all depends on the individual. I say that you can, since I am able to! And I'm not the only one.

Pauty: Every country has had its "children of the age," who have all wept over the wreckage of a failed revolution. . . .

Calaferte: I don't really dream of revolution. What I dream is of a quiet revolution. *L'Homme vivant* is the breviary of the quiet revolution: one says no, that's all. One doesn't do anything. I don't plant bombs, I don't incite riots. I say *no,* but a firm *no.* And when I say *no* it means *no.* It is the *weapon of refusal.*

Utopia exists. Utopia is useful to the extent that if I am utopian, if you are utopian, if your brother, your cousin, your friend, your partner are utopian, then that constitutes a group. From that point on, ideas can change, probably at an intellectual level, but if ideas change, be it ever so little, at a truly intellectual level, then things will necessarily change as well.

I don't accept politics. I don't need men telling me what to do when I get up in the morning. I must make my own decisions. That's all I want to say on the subject of political man.

Pauty: If men had not stupidly submitted to politics, we would not have arrived at horrors like the Holocaust. At the Nuremberg trials, all the directors of the death camps used the same defense: "I obeyed orders."

A man must know that he is responsible for his acts and disobey if he does not want to be complicit in such tragedies?

Calaferte: He must know how to say *no.*

Pauty: Have you seen those pictures from the former Yugoslavia: armed men, clutching crucifixes, setting out for some ethnic purification with the priests' blessing?

Calaferte: Twenty centuries this has been going on! Twenty centuries! There must be a stop put to these pressurings from the church! Be it Catholic, Protestant, Orthodox, Islamic, Buddhist, or whatever else.

It is absolutely necessary that the individual possess a strong sense of religion, of the very essence of religion, to stop these pressurings on the part of the church. This little intellectual paradox merits explanation. If we don't start with this refusal, which reflects a desire for clarity, for a return to sources, a return to childhood innocence—I myself often have the wish that I may die innocent, it's my only ambition—if we don't embark on this course soon, our societies will be faced with two eventualities: war, the usual war that is familiar to all our political states, whatever their governments; or internal strife such as will inevitably lead us back to dictatorships, to Nazism. And as long as Nazism is possible, we are still under oppression!

Pauty: Those terrible images of the Iran-Iraq war come to mind: thousands of men killed, machine-gunned, gassed, each with a piece of paper on his person, a certificate granting him entry to paradise. Ecclesiastics had manipulated them into joining another holy war.

Calaferte: First, knowledge. Second, explanation.

Explanation is important because there are unspeakable duperies in our societies. Those who do the duping, the manipulators, have the media on their side, the word, and they have propagandists in their service, since we are still under propagandist regimes. Let us never forget that! Propaganda disguised as information. Some would have us believe that we live in the communications age! There has never been less communicated than today! Do you happen to know who the great writers of Greece, Norway, or Albania are currently? No, you don't, and if you did it would only be by accident.

Pauty: Are you implying that there is a sort of cabal against knowledge on the part of those in power? A cabal that would work against the development of individuality within the polis?

Calaferte: Undoubtedly. Who is it that opposes those in power? The individual.

Pauty: Knowledge, then, is something the individual must seek out on his own?

Calaferte: It's preferable if he has help. I am thinking of knowledge gained through initiation, through solidarity, through the intermediary of a generous initiation, by which I mean one that is free, something my wife and I are trying to do.

Pauty: You take care of children?

Calaferte: Yes.

Pauty: I wanted to hear you say that specifically, because some of your detractors identify you with an antisocial form of Christianity.

Calaferte: My Christianity is very simple: I feel myself to be a creature in a universe, in a cosmogony without beginning or end, as the Scriptures say so well. I think that I have been, that I am, that I will be. I believe I have necessity, a purpose. In all honesty I don't know exactly what it is, but I must have one just as the ant has one, just as that pigeon does, the one pecking at food here in front of us. I believe we must serve what is happy—happy and good in the world—because there is also Evil. Evil exists. Dark forces are in action, as you can observe on any day.

Religious symbolism describes this from the beginning of

Genesis. Cain and Abel, they are a perfectly clear symbol. Cain's offerings are not accepted by God. Later on this will be taken up again by Christ, who said: "Make it such that their eyes not open, lest they see, and their ears not hear, lest they understand." This is to divide. Purely and simply to divide. Now why this dividing?

the dark forces

....

Jean-Pierre Pauty: Examine the Book of Job carefully and you discover the existence of a sort of pact. It isn't God who tempts Job, but Satan who proposes to God that he test Job's faith.

Louis Calaferte: What is Evil is Evil, and what is Good is Good. Each of us knows what is Good and what is Evil for himself. Both in our conscience and in the world around us.

Pauty: They are going to accuse you of Manichaeanism.

Calaferte: I couldn't care less. I note that certain currents are diabolical, and certain others beneficent. That's what I see.

Pauty: The Cathars, who leaned toward the Manichaean, who stressed "the sin of the flesh"—their position is a long way from yours.

Calaferte: Their position is a very long way from mine. The principle underlying, no matter what religion, is always the same: each is based on oppression and sectarianism. I'm talking about religions, not the religious spirit within us, and that is an important distinction. For me, what makes the religious is the individual's relationship with his God.

No churches, no chapels, no mosques, no cathedrals. Just a man alone with his God. This is what the initiate whom we know as Christ—and I see him above all as an initiate—says to you again and again: when you want to pray to your Father, shut yourself in your own room.[1] That's all. When you want something—and this is where the miracle of grace comes into it—Christ doesn't say gather with three thousand others on a public square, he says let two of you pray, if two of you are of one mind and agree to ask for something—which is extremely difficult, much more so than people think. If two of you are of one mind and agree to ask for something, you'll obtain it.

We are returning to the magical universe of Hebraic civilization, of ancient civilizations generally. I believe that man possesses his own powers, which the powers-that-be have eroded. Magic lies outside the realm of worldly power, outside systems. Magic is the love of God inside us. There is a real force there. I want to be very modest, I don't want to talk about such things as these, but I do want to say that I have felt and experienced it myself two or three times in my life. I know what I am talking about.

Pauty: Taking the forces of evil into account was something that the writer Georges Bataille strongly believed in. Bataille even regretted that the important role of the devil in eroticism has been lessened: "One of the signs of this decline is the slight amount of attention paid nowadays to the devil: people believe in him less and less, one feels moved to say not at all. This means that the dark sacred, more ill defined than ever, finally loses all meaning. The domain of the sacred is reduced to that of the God of Good, whose realm ends where the light stops: nothing remains in this domain that is accursed."[2] If I understand correctly, you feel it is important to locate, to isolate, this "accursed element." Do you believe certain men are more inhabited than others by this spirit?

Calaferte: To begin with, I want to say that these words you have just quoted of Georges Bataille's are altogether remarkable. They are the words of someone who is not a theoretician but a man of experience. I believe and I am convinced that certain persons are more inhabited than others by the spirit of Evil; experience shows this to be so.

Each of us knows, more or less, what he is potentially capable of. Each of us obscurely knows how he will react, how he will behave, even in exceptional, or violent, or actually tragic circumstances. I'm not saying we always hold to the line, since we aren't all black or all white. But as regards the great essentials, there is a certain direction laid down in the world for things to follow. That is the x-direction. And then there is another direction, and things are equally meant to take that course. That's the y-direction. One may certainly ask why. I don't have an answer. It isn't to be found anywhere. . . .

Heraclitus said, "The world is made through friction." This is an extremely profound statement.

Pauty: Then there are men who embody these powers?

Calaferte: There are the reprobates, the damned; and there are the others. So why are they damned?

Pauty: That's terrible!

Calaferte: It's terrible, yes and no. It's terrible in a psychological judgment. If the individual is beheld from the perspective of psychology it is indeed terrible. And this perspective has been ours since the middle of the eighteenth century. Even in school—and I have examples of this—children are still being taught exclusively in terms of psychological reality. But if we stopped classifying people according to the logic of psychology and replaced it with that of metaphysics, if we could learn to look at men not as psychological entities but as destinies, then whole sections of our thought would fall away and new directions open up.

When Christ says, for instance, "Thou shalt not judge," we may, a priori, say it's impossible—if our standpoint remains that of psychology—but if we shift to a metaphysical standpoint, if I behold you as a destiny, and you in turn behold me as a destiny, then the act of passing judgment is silly. There is simply no point in doing it! Whereas if you are judging a psychology you can say "He acted badly," or "She did this," or "She did that." But if a person is "like this" or "like that" what you are talking about is the whole of a destiny. The person is "like this" or "like that" in order to fulfill a certain destiny. And that person wouldn't fulfill it the way he's going to fulfill it if he were different. The things that pertain to human beings must be viewed on a strictly metaphysical plane, leaving psychology entirely aside.

Pauty: You mean there is no way of explaining the case of Rimbaud unless you look at him from the point of view of a destiny? No explanation for the influence of his work over the last hundred years, when he himself thought that it had been burned, left unread?

Calaferte: Rimbaud was a genius. There is nothing maleficent about a genius. Nothing. A sort of grace surrounds the genius. His strength tends naturally toward rebellion, a rebellion against what is visible, in other words society. So a boy genius of thirteen or fourteen or sixteen is necessarily going to be in a state of re-bellion, in a state where he perforce says no to everything. And in this state he will repudiate the divine as well. The process is perfectly comprehensible, but society is the cause of it—the social, in the form of misfortune, Misfortune with a capital *M*. Subsequently to that, something is achieved, which, to put it simply, is the work. It extends over a long period or a short one. With Rimbaud, the work was accomplished in a flash.

I don't believe that genius, at least to my knowledge, has ever emanated from dark forces. Talent is a different matter.

Pauty: The question of the genius—of a Rimbaud or a Mozart —the question of predestination: these present a problem for rationalists and materialists. Why is that?

Calaferte: I think our texts say it, but so do the others—the *Bhagavad Gita,* and so on. It's perfectly clear: "Man does not live by bread alone." If that's the case, if he doesn't live by bread alone, then he must be given something else and there need to be people to give that something else to him.

Let it be repeated once again: society has falsified the fact of art. It has become a commercial act, the product of ambition, a source of vanity. A man devotes himself to an artistic task—whatever it be, whether large or small—but one in which his entire life is engaged (I'm not talking about art as a distraction, or about your Sunday painter, for example), and this artistic task is necessarily going to concern, going to affect, one or two or three or ten other people. The artist is "destined." He is only an intermediary and nothing more. There is nothing to be vain about here. I once proposed publishing my books without an author's credit. They told me I was crazy. But I'm not crazy at all. I sense things, and I know now, having reached my present age, that I was destined for such and such accomplishments and that my writings, as you have very kindly said, have on occasion been useful to others. That's it.

I am to such a point a mere intermediary—both in writing and painting—that I am incapable of remaking something once it has been made. I am no longer able to. The work is something that has been sent to me. I look upon this as a favor from on high, for it's true that it affords you immensely privileged moments—for which, materially speaking, you subsequently have to pay.

I am sixty-five years old, I am poor, but I have the dignity, the contentment, and the joy of poverty. My wife and I have a motto: "We don't have a dime, but we're fine." I don't ask for anything else. Now as to the question of election and of reprobation, that's something else again.

Pauty: That's a crucial question. Have you seen Milos Forman's film about Mozart, *Amadeus*?

Calaferte: Yes, I've seen it. Its somewhat rudimentary aspects aside, the film does a good job of showing how a man who is not inspired can become infuriated when faced with the joyful madness of the person who is. I don't say that an inspired man isn't visited by doubts, doesn't suffer. There is also the uncertainty of youth, the terrible uncertainty of the present moment, and of the future, which wouldn't exist if it were not for this social oppression. All right, you would say to yourself, I'm an artist, period. Sure, there are taxes to pay, and the rent, etc., but all of that is in the social world. You shouldn't mix everything, but simply assume your fate to the extent you can. If you can't assume it, you endure its constraints. But inside you are nonetheless a force, an incredible force. And it has an effect on others. It becomes recognized. And it also sometimes provokes a violent hatred in others, which we all know about! That's the story of every artist.

Pauty: The capacity to create is for you a gift of God?

Calaferte: The capacity to create is God given. There is no instance where it has been anything else.

Pauty: Even when Nietzsche writes *The Antichrist* and declares that God is dead?

Calaferte: He wanted to give himself an explanation. You know, in the exalted state inspiration brings on, you sometimes want to substitute yourself for the All. You feel invulnerable. That has happened to me.

Pauty: Isn't that what we call the temptation of the demiurge? The Promethean temptation that precedes a fall. Stealing fire from the gods. The temptation that with Rimbaud decrees the poet as a "stealer of the fire."

Calaferte: It is the feeling of knowing, obscurely, that one is destined to something, and that nothing is going to halt it. And nothing does.

Pauty: Did you have these metaphysical intimations from a very young age?

Calaferte: Yes. Long before I was eighteen.

Pauty: Then how is it there is no sign of this in your early books? Why does it only start to appear with *Septentrion*?

Calaferte: I didn't address these problems because I wasn't certain about my thinking.

Pauty: You say you feel yourself at a great distance from your first books, that they are settlings of accounts.

Calaferte: Yes. I went through a period of violent negation, very, very intense, when I developed crushing arguments, for instance, to describe Christ as an alcoholic. Yes, I had that period. . . .

But I was rapidly confronted. . . . When I was about sixteen, I was confronted . . . but I don't want to talk about it. I came upon reality, the reality that is mine today and that will follow me until the end of time.

Every individual who is born is a force. There's a force unleashed in the world. There's a kind of seizure of power, a seizing of place.

A baby, from the moment of its birth, occupies a volume in the world. Consequently it's a disturbance. It disturbs molecules. If the child wails, or moves, it upsets the way things are, destroys chains of molecules. Once it starts speaking, it occupies a place that was empty—its own place in the world. And that place has its meaning, its significance—a molecular, not a psychological one.

That this individual has deployed force of a certain quality, at a certain moment, at a determined point in space-time— I underscore the word *determined*—that is the issue. When a child dies at the age of two and an old man dies at ninety-two, the system of forces remains the same; only the duration differs, but the determination that called for it has been accomplished. So what has been accomplished? That is the real question. Molecular disturbances, probably, molecular processes that have a primordial meaning. Again, Heraclitus said "The world is made through friction." And again we are outside the logic of psychology. I think, for example, that in our interview the essential thing is not what is being said. The essential thing is what is going on around us, what is going on in your mind, in mine, what we are disturbing, what we are shifting about, what we are putting back in order without knowing it.

Pauty: You are making almost the same argument as Stephen Hawking, who produced a kind of Big Bang in the rationalist world of science by saying that there was an underlying order behind things: "The whole history of science has been the gradual realization that events do not happen in an arbitrary manner, but that they reflect a certain underlying order, which may or may not be divinely inspired. . . . Because energy cannot be created out of nothing, one of the particles in a particle/antiparticle pair will have positive energy, and the other partner negative energy."[3]

Calaferte: I wasn't aware of that. As for the death of the infant or the death of the old man, it results in an equivalence. A force was released to accomplish something at a determined moment in space-time. No one gets very upset at the death of an old man; they say, "Well he was old, he had a good long life." Yet people are greatly upset when a child dies, to the extent that they have made entirely hypothetical projections regarding it. But hasn't the child accomplished what it was meant to accomplish?

Pauty: To such an idea of predestination, some might raise the objection of the Holocaust.

Calaferte: Violent dark forces have very often been unleashed in the course of man's history.

I am going to say something terrible: I think there can be

holocausts through the absence of an awakened conscience on the part of each individual.

Pauty: Do you mean that if we continue to ignore what is happening in Eastern Europe and allow it to continue, it might resurface on our doorstep?

Calaferte: In Eastern Europe and elsewhere, in Western Europe even. We are one and all allowing things to happen that we will have to pay for very probably in a painful and violent way.

Pauty: Because everything accumulates, layer on layer?

Calaferte: Because everything accumulates and creates systems of force. I call them dark forces. Call them light green forces if you like.

Pauty: Do you mean chthonian forces?

Calaferte: They are subterranean forces. Dark forces. And there are those who are willing to serve them. Their troops are ready. . . .

Pauty: The current discourse of historians is practically in agreement with you. They think that Hitler's aim was not solely to destroy the Jews, but that, had he been able to, he would have destroyed all humankind. He would have destroyed his entire people, the children, everyone.

Calaferte: This is a new discourse that I wasn't aware of, but it certainly took them long enough to arrive at the realization! In the end you clearly have to adopt a metaphysical understanding of the world and stop thinking that the world is an accident!

Everywhere there are satanic forces ready to serve. Witnesses like the writer Sébastien Mercier, in the eighteenth century, at the beginning of the French Revolution, were surprised to encounter certain groups in the streets. . . . I myself, in Lyons, on the eve of the May '68 uprisings, saw gangs at two o'clock in the morning, menacing gangs, wearing black leather gloves, gangs you would never see abroad normally. The chthonian forces rise out of the earth. . . . In symbolic terms, you are obviously seeing the action of fire, just as you see it exert itself during wars. It is no coincidence that language makes use of this word to designate the bringers of death, *firearms*. There is an Arab proverb of profound traditional and symbolic significance that says: "The devil makes the guns."

There is a purifying fire and a destroying fire. The destroying fire is the fire of death, the satanic fire. We have seen it in action.

Pauty: The Holocaust?

Calaferte: Let there be no ambiguity! The people who died by fire were victims of these dark forces. When I talk of fire, I do so in relation to the whole of religious symbology. When we're dealing with historical facts, then we come to what I call in my jargon "the aggregate victim of the dark forces." The aggregate victim of the dark forces refers to everything that has been sacrificed to the profit of these same dark forces.

Here it is not a question of election or of reprobation. This is a historical fact, the consequence of what might be called nonrefusal on the part of each and every one of us. We are unfortunately all responsible. It's too easy to always make others responsible! We are responsible too!

Today, in other circumstances, the question may arise again. It is important to know that, faced with Evil, we have the weapon of refusal. The victims of Evil are not the victims of God. They are the victims of Evil.

Those military powers were led by men, it mustn't be forgotten! And who were those men? The men of the new German army: the SS.

Pauty: Who proudly displayed symbols of death on their uniforms.

Calaferte: Symbols of satanism! The death's head, the eagle, and the twin lightning bolts worn by the SS on their sleeves were perfectly clear symbols. The black and silver of their uniforms are those of the drapes in mortuary ceremonies. Black and silver, they're the cemetery. And when you add that behind all this was a secret society called the Synarchy . . .

I recently revisited the Museum of the Deportation in Besançon, a remarkably conceived museum, very oppressive. You can see there a large photograph of the women guards at the Bergen-Belsen concentration camp. There are about ten of them in the picture. I looked at them individually, one after the other. They all have demonic features. All of them, without exception. They are smiling, and they are frightening. I also had another chance to see the photograph of Hindenburg shaking hands with a completely obsequious Hitler. Right next to it is a photograph of Hitler giving a speech, utterly transformed into a demon.

Pauty: There are numerous photographs where you see Hitler trying out poses, different attitudes for later, seeking for the gesture, the look, that will magnetize the crowds.

Calaferte: A history of Nazism could be made using only photographs . . . with every known aspect of satanism: seduction, obsequiousness, deviousness, violence.

Pauty: At the end of the Book of Job, Job recovers his faith, having become conscious of the duality of the world (Yahweh/Satan).

Man can resist Evil to the extent that he believes in these two opposing forces?

Calaferte: That's the whole question. But let us be clear on it: you, I, each one of us is able to resist.

The spirit of murder is not in me, the spirit of hate is not in me, so I am not a satanic auxiliary. You must declare who you are and say that Evil is Evil. Our societies behave as though Evil did not exist. They hush it up. Nazism, which is, after all, Evil carried to the absolute, and Evil believed in absolutely, was practiced in the cellars. It didn't happen in broad daylight. It happened inside isolated places, closed off behind barbed wire, guarded by dogs.

Pauty: It wasn't from shame, a guilty conscience?

Calaferte: Not at all! Evil is afraid of being unable to act. It knows very well in what areas it can act. That's why I often talk about chthonian forces. They are dark forces, hidden forces. Evil is wary, it hides. Don't think that Evil is ashamed, it's afraid! That's why it has to be flushed out and firmly accused. You can't be hesitant in dealing with Evil, you have to be firm.

Evil is Evil, Good is Good. I come back to that again because it's important in my thought. Evil is not "reasonable," it is entirely unreasonable. You have to know that Evil is unreason. So you can't oppose it with reason and think that it will spare us. When Evil is set in motion somewhere, it is set in motion for everyone, that too is something you must know.

You must not bend down to it, you must confront it, knowing it is Evil and denouncing it.

Pauty: That brings up the question of conscience, the awakening of conscience.

Calaferte: I think that the lesser satanic auxiliaries don't know very exactly what they are doing within the overall action. I can offer some proof of this. In Germany during the war, the SS committed all sorts of villainies. When it came time for the general annihilation of the Jews, for putting the system in place—the trucks, the gas chambers, the crematories—certain of the SS refused. They committed suicide. Others ended up in the hospital, in mental wards, half crazy. So there is reason to believe that at some point there was an awakening of conscience. It is this awakening of conscience on the part of the servants, the auxiliaries of Evil, that allows Good to carry the day. That's how the process works, in my opinion.

Pauty: C. G. Jung deplored the fact that we have forgotten, lost, the knowledge of the alchemists—the symbolic image, paradox, the studies of matter: "The great problem of psychology is the reintegration of opposites; this recurs everywhere and on every level. Already in my *Psychology and Alchemy,* I had occasion to deal with the integration of 'Satan.' For as long as Satan is not integrated, the world is not cured and man is not saved. But Satan represents evil, and how can evil be integrated? There is only one possibility: to assimilate it, meaning to raise it to the level of consciousness. That is what is called in alchemy the Conjunction of the Two Principles." [4]

Calaferte: Without wanting to disparage anyone else, I believe that Jung represents the very great thought of our time. He understood perfectly that the origin of the individual and of all living things is in essence metaphysical, divinized, satanized.

Pauty: Thanks to his knowledge of the symbols from the past, he was among the first to detect in the dreams of his patients the gathering horrors of the last world war, of fascism.

Calaferte: When we say that something was "in the air," what do we mean by that? For one thing, that your neighbor is expressing something. Something beneficial or something harmful, but he is expressing it! Popular language has ways of saying this: "you could feel it coming," "you knew it was going to happen," etc. How did you know it? You knew it individually. In certain individuals, dreams are the reflectors, the sensitive plate recording past, present, and future events.

Jung was very struck by this ascending of chthonian forces. He was practicing during the pre-Nazi era, so it is hardly surprising. A few years back, I saw an exhibit of German expressionists—work from 1908 to 1912—and the paintings very clearly foretell the Nazism that was on its way. There are engravings, black and white drawings, that are almost adumbrations of the concentration camps that were to appear thirty or thirty-five years later. So in certain cases, as you were just saying about Rimbaud, the artist is a "seer." But I think also that each of us is a seer. This isn't generally known or said. We are seers in diurnal life and seers in nocturnal life.

The nineteenth century was catastrophic inasmuch as it did away with miraculous life, magical life. Today, we live only in accordance with "physical" parameters, "organizing" parameters. When everything collapses, there is no explanation. People just say, "Yes, it collapsed, they made a mistake somewhere."

Except for the Orient and black Africa, the entire world now lives according to a single light: the supremacy of the will of the individual. But can a person be born when and as he chooses? The whole problem lies there. If the answer is yes then all right, everything I have to say is false! But I stress: as he wants, as the individual himself wants, and not as someone else wants, a manipulator or a doctor, because in that case, it is not the individual who has decided to be born. The day the individual can decide to be born, all my theories will have to be revised. But as long as the individual cannot be born as he himself wants, the supremacy of his will, of the will of the individual, has not been shown.

Pauty: I would like to return to the theme of war. You say that since 1914 there has been a kind of acceleration, less and less respect for man, for life.

Calaferte: Louis Guilloux put it in a nutshell: "The year 1917 inaugurated the time of the assassins." The First World War still resembled what all wars had been like up to that time: barbarous, and medieval, with all their horseshit, their sense of honor, etc. What has "the sense of honor" to do with war, with murder?

Guilloux saw what was happening: we were becoming mired in a world of assassins! There is even a writer like Herr Ernst Jünger, whom I abhor, who made a career out of being in the German army before and after World War I, and who mentions this difference between the two world wars, the difference in mental outlook between the soldier in 1914 and the soldier in 1940. He was a determined and obstinate warrior, though, which is why I care so little for him—even if I recognize his talents as a writer.

Pauty: Guilloux's phrase is in fact based on an earlier phrase by Rimbaud: "Now is the time of the assassins," which Henry Miller picked up and used it as the title of his essay on Rimbaud, in which he forecast that the loss of spirituality in the modern world would bring about worse horrors even than the two world wars: "Today the loss of faith is universal. Here God himself is powerless. We have put our faith in the bomb, and it is the bomb which will answer our prayers."[5]

When the book appeared after the Second World War, no one could understand why Miller was predicting a new apocalypse, more murderous than the one before. . . .

Calaferte: That is why is one must constantly stress the act of understanding:

1. Explanation
2. Knowledge
3. Absorbing the world

Knowing who one is, why one is, how one is. That's not a Utopia. It's possible. It's all I preach. I don't preach anything else.

Pauty: In *L'Homme vivant* you advocate the weapon of refusal. I quote: "Know that there is the weapon of refusal. Refusal is a spiritual weapon. If refusal engenders violence around you, then withdraw. But afterward go back to refusing. What is obtained in this way will have been procured with the only true and insurmountable force, the force of the Spirit."

Calaferte: I advocate the weapon of refusal and the denunciation of Evil—the denunciation of Evil from its inception! One must not wait for it to take hold and ramify, because once Evil has made its spiderweb, flies will get caught in it, that's obvious.

As soon as you see the spider, you have to say to yourself, Look out! In a little while we'll have a web. And today I say: "Look out, there's going to be a web." That is why my mental state is one of refusal, my political state is one of refusal, my social state is one of refusal. I would like to be proven wrong, I would like for there to be no spider at all; but as things appear to me . . .

Pauty: The twenty-first century will be more barbarous than the twentieth?

Calaferte: Yes. . . . And the twentieth isn't over yet. The germ of this evil is a germ of hate, which is called Nazism. Nazism is a religion, let's make no mistake about it. And as a religion it can still engender giant catastrophes. Whether they are owned up to or not. I don't think that today anyone would announce it openly: "I am a Nazi, here I come." But in sweetened, palatable forms, Evil exists.

Evil can be of use to governments, because we are in an age of massification that entails unemployment, regression, recession. And what is their solution? War. And war is Evil.

Pauty: Doesn't the fact of Nazism taking root during periods of crisis explain why certain individuals, who are anxious, uncertain about the future, or who have nothing to lose or to hope for, should be prepared to fall into line behind anyone and anything, losing all sense of values and all conscience?

Calaferte: No. Nazism makes its bed in the heart of man. In the heart of certain men. Whether a time of crisis or not, Nazism occurs wherever the dark forces are ready to act.

# of spiritual factors

....

Jean-Pierre Pauty: Concerning what you call the oppression exercised by ecclesiastical institutions, the German theologian and psychotherapist Eugen Drewermann has just been excommunicated for having raised questions about church dogma, for having interpreted miracles as symbols in his books and lectures. I would like to know if you, Louis Calaferte, believe in miracles.

Louis Calaferte: I believe in miracles because life itself is a miracle.

To open my eyes each morning, to be constituted as I am, that is really a pure miracle. That I should have a mind that has been functioning for sixty years, to me that is a miracle. I believe in a miraculous daily life. I'm not talking about apparitions, about more or less hallucinatory visions, phenomena I have little interest in. What interests me is the consciousness of a miraculous life, that is, the possibility for an individual to be in contact with what is beyond him. With God or with something else, call it what you will, but in contact with what lies beyond us.

Pauty: When Christ walks on water, isn't that a symbol?

Calaferte: I don't interpret it that way but as the act of an initiate who has accumulated the necessary forces to achieve mastery on the purely physical plane. I am unable to walk on water, but then neither am I an initiate. What I can do, and what each of us can do with regard to the various states, the various situations in our lives—if we have a certain faith in the absolute, in the unity of this world—is that we can transcend, and we can do so almost every day. That's the miraculous.

I personally have problems getting up from a chair, but when I choose to gather a certain kind of force inside me, I manage to get up. That's "Arise and walk." It seems to me to be the meaning of life. We have forgotten it. We continue to forget it. As long as we forget it we will remain inferior to what we are in reality capable of being. Psychoanalysis has also grasped this very clearly.

Pauty: Your perspective is quite close to Drewermann's: "I nonetheless believe that Jesus walked on water and that he continues to do so. Torn between fear and confidence, it is always up to us to decide to find out whether the world is an abyss. . . . Depending on our answer, we will sink or feel the water bearing our weight. This is what faith is. . . . For the world is full of miracles. Yet for that to be so one must be prepared to accept them symbolically." [1] The church, for which Christ's resurrection is key, rejected Drewermann's symbolic interpretation, according to which the resurrection is the symbol of man's resurrection in his own life. Is the resurrection a key thing for you?

Calaferte: I do not see it as key. I think that I too have been raised from the dead. That we have all been raised from the dead, and that we will all be resurrected on various occasions. It will happen in the coming millennia. For me, it is drawing near. I am going to die and I am going to be resurrected—according to our present-day terminology and concepts, for it must be admitted that our concepts are very, very rationalist.

As to the resurrection of Christ, I don't want to pronounce on it. It can obviously be explained symbolically—the number three, the third day, the presence of the women who are there to witness the resurrection, to mention only the main points. There is a whole symbolic aspect to the resurrection. Whether or not Christ rose from the grave, whether he was resurrected or not, this seems less important to me than to know intellectually that each day we are ourselves a resurrection, that we daily undergo the resurrection ourselves and that we have to maintain ourselves in a state of resurrection, which is a state of life, a state of happiness, a state of determination to be and not of living sacrifice.

If I become so heated on the subject of the churches it is because they teach us the "sacrificial" line. We are to be sacrificial beings. Our grandmothers are purported to have sinned somewhere along the way. I have trouble accepting this. Whether the Resurrection is or is not purely symbolic matters little to me intellectually; and the same holds for the Ascension. Of course, I believe that there is a whole realm of symbols. But the phenomenon of the Resurrection is perhaps in one's own flesh as well. That is an area where it is hard to give answers. I don't like to "float" in realms that I don't have a feeling of, that I don't know, that I have not been able to interpret myself. When speaking of these problems, you shouldn't stray from the logic of thought to which your experience entitles you. As far as I myself am concerned, it's true that I visualize my own resurrection on the symbolic plane. That is enough for me in that it allows me to feel practically invulnerable, in that it allows me to feel that I am "outliving the times." I can say, therefore, that there is for me a constant, permanent resurrection. Christ's was an "accident," physically. Yes, it's possible, why not, but it makes no difference to the essence of being, to "is-ness."

Pauty: At the end of your book *Septentrion*, the protagonist undergoes a sort of rebirth. Do you place his experience in the category of *co-naissance*, a spiritual and intellectual rebirth?

Calaferte: Yes. Now we are getting into particulars. It was a transformation. Fate rules over transformations, in my opinion, and the will plays little part in them. What is, must be; and what is, is. Thought comes afterward, and only afterward can you set down in a book the work that has taken place within you.

The writing of *Septentrion* was very long. The book took me five years to write because the transformation occurring inside me was immense. I realized this much later.

The writing of that book corresponded to a deep inner laceration—not a mental laceration—a slash of lightning across the sky, a great cosmic tearing apart. I don't think *Septentrion* can be considered an intellectual work. I wasn't aiming at that. I am not basically an intellectual. I am someone who thinks, who absorbs life to the maximum, who tries to apprehend life as abundantly, as broadly as possible.

In *Septentrion* there was an attempt to be delivered of something that had been a part of me but would subsequently cease to be. That book transformed me completely. It was a break, a trench opened in my existence. You could call it a kind of exorcism, but I don't see any point in that. The term I prefer is a therapeutic liquidation.

It was also the moment when I met people who taught me things. It was the time in my life when I changed myself. It was also then that I started to live with the person who is today my

Louis Calaferte with his wife, Guillemette. Lyons, 1976. (Photograph, collection G. Calaferte)

wife. There was a total change. I was a nomad and would probably have remained one had there not been that encounter. Ultimately, a table and some paper are all I need on the material plane. I can perfectly well live in a corner with a little table and some paper, that is my underlying nature. The fact of being sedentary sometimes weighs painfully on me. I need to feel that I am a nomad, all that is bound up with my origins. . . .

Pauty: When the protagonist in *Septentrion*, who is in fact yourself, undergoes a sort of epiphany in front of Dali's *Christ,* then chances upon the book by Kierkegaard that talks about a man choosing his direction in life—was this a novelistic invention or something that actually happened?

Calaferte: It is not an invention. In *Septentrion* there isn't even any literary structure.

Pauty: You hadn't made an outline?

Calaferte: I don't make outlines. I write when the good Lord wants me to write. The idea of an outline is completely foreign to me.

I didn't decide one day to make a career for myself as a writer. One day, I have no idea why or how, I said to myself: "You are going to be a writer." I was twelve or thirteen. I didn't know a thing. I hadn't read a thing. I was working in a factory. Even then I thought of writing—of practicing any art—as a "grace," as something God given and sacred. I haven't changed my attitude, I still feel the same way today and am very glad I do. That is my position with regard to the creative act, it is very simple. I don't think of anything in particular, the pressures grow and at a certain moment these pressures have to explode.

Pauty: Yet, reading *Septentrion,* it does seem to have a very specific structure.

Calaferte: No, I divided it into three parts after writing it.

Pauty: The story-within-a-story aspect is not deliberate?

Calaferte: No. I'll even make a confession to you. . . . It has been true all my life as a writer and continues to be as true now as ever: *I wait.* I wait, that's all. When I was younger and less assured of this phenomenon, I had moments of great depression, of very great doubt, bordering on difficult mental attitudes.

These were very painful moments, when I would think that I was no longer authorized to create—and that could have been so. In time, I came to understand that there are great expanses containing nothing at all, and I accepted that.

Today I know that my accumulated store of experimentings with life, with others, with looking at others, with paying attention to others, that this accumulation gives me the sense at sixty-five of there still being things I have to say.

Whether I will be able to say them, whether I will be given the manner of saying them, I have no idea. I don't know how to describe myself. I am neither a technician nor a calculator. I wait. I think that defines it best.

Pauty: If, as you believe, one is destined to write, then how do you explain that Rimbaud was able to renounce writing, the act of writing, otherwise than of his own will?

Calaferte: I don't believe that will plays any part in art. I have written somewhere: "All calculation in art ends in error." I'm convinced of it. With these people who calculate their effects, it always leads to vapid work. There are three million examples of it.

As to Rimbaud, there was so much lightning in him that its discharge came very soon; that cape once rounded, there was only death. This goes for Mozart and a few others as well. The lightning discharges.

It is truly lightning, not the "mirror." Something bursts. Rimbaud, like Mozart, is a victim of his own explosion.

Pauty: Other fundamentally spiritual authors—Berdyaev, Kierkegaard, Chestov—have preceded you in expressing this metaphysical, mystical, and religious view of the world. In one of his works Benjamin Fondane named this view of things the "unhappy consciousness." Would you accept this as a denomination for your own thought?

Calaferte: The unhappy consciousness is never creative, ever. A consciousness prey to doubt is creative; so is a questing consciousness, which is the case with Kierkegaard. But the point is crucial: one must be in quest.

It is not a question of having certainties, but of having directions to find and of following them as honestly as possible.

Talk of an "unhappy consciousness" strikes me as the projection of a mind with no experience of the spiritual. When I encounter this sort of thinking, I just let people talk, I don't respond.

Pauty: Even if I tell you that "the mystical is no more than a crutch for man"?

Calaferte: I could answer that it's better to walk leaning on a crutch than not to walk at all.

What is man? That's the whole question! Despite what may be said by materialists, by atheists, by rationalists, by agnostics, etc.—I'm not formulating criticisms, I respect freedom of thought, everyone thinks what he likes—so with due respect to all those people, man taken as a whole, if one is willing to think about that whole, remains a huge mystery, along with the entirety of creation. Why does a seed have the future blossom inside it? For my part I don't know. Every rational, scientific, or explanatory answer seems to me to fall short of the question. If some people can be content with that, good for them. But when they qualify the mystical and spiritual approach to the world as a crutch, I for my part take that to be the true infirmity in which the vast majority of our contemporaries are steeped. An infirmity that results in this world of cruelty, mindlessness, and metaphysical Evil, with a capital *E*.

Pauty: That reminds me of a passage from your pamphlet *Droit de cité:*

> Massification, bringing with it the weight of economic factors. An imperative inevitably leading to:
>   1. the banalization of the mediocre
>   2. the legitimization of the mediocre
>   3. the glorification of the mediocre.
>
> Newspapers, television, theater, film, songs, novels, food, the hotel trade, the fashion in clothing, and, consequently, human relations—nothing escapes the pressure, from which quantities of people benefit more or less directly.
>
> Could it be possible that one fine day we will hear talk of *spiritual* factors?

Calaferte: I am entirely for providing people with the flour they need so they can eat, but at the same time I would like someone to tell them: "We're giving you the flour, but it doesn't end there:

you have to take stock of the origin of this poverty." There are reasons for poverty, and massification is not solely responsible. Great poverty and famines do not occur accidentally.

Pauty: The destruction of certain living forces of nature does not happen simply by chance?

Calaferte: Material interest, profit! And this profit goes with names, the names of the companies that have exploited black Africa, that are turning South America into a desert, where the population will have to face gigantic famines. Behind these companies stand policies, politicians, we can rapidly get hold of their names, if you like. This propensity to profit, to exploitation, has nothing to do with spiritualist behavior, but everything to do with materialism.

In Europe, we are far from experiencing such poverty, but there are nonetheless warning signs of a state of decomposition.

islands
of prayer

Jean-Pierre Pauty: You told me one day that you believe in the force of prayer. Can a prayer have an effect on the world?

Louis Calaferte: Yes. Unfortunately, the churches have queered everything! Prayer is a magical act. Prayer obtains what it is due to obtain—not what I personally want to obtain, which is different. It is useful that islands of prayer exist in the world, even if they are composed of only one person, or two, or three, or four.

The state of prayer is a state of force. It is an axis. When you pray, you are in an axial position. The axial position is a position of force that lies waiting. Like a reservoir. Like a crucible. One day it will rain, the reservoir will fill, forces will accrue.

From the moment a person, whoever he may be, is in an axial position, that person is "untouchable" and draws forces toward him. One mustn't interpret prayer foolishly. The texts tell us so: tirelessly repeating thousands of words is to no purpose, for God knows what you need. He knows it in advance, and there is no point in asking him for it; but there are distinctions to be drawn. There are states of prayer that are penetrating, you can sense it, you can tell, and there are states of prayer that penetrate nothing at all, that are a kind of repetitiousness.

Pauty: The prayer wheels of the Buddhist religion?

Calaferte: Prayer wheels are something else. Sound enters into it, the ritual of sound. Sound propagates and of itself creates molecular zones into which certain forces can penetrate.

The excellence of prayer is in creating a vacuum. Elsewhere there is no possibility of a vacuum. As soon as there is one, it is immediately filled.

Through prayer we obtain fabulous things, but according to my view these fabulous things have been obtained already even before you have begun prayers to obtain them. Prayer is in itself above all acknowledgment, the implicit acknowledgment of the fact that everything has been obtained, that everything has been so ordered that things conspire toward your fulfillment in a determined direction. You ask for what you already possess.

Pauty: In this you are in agreement with a writer you have a particular fondness for and whom you have often quoted in your *Carnets*, one of the great mystical figures of the century, the writer Simone Weil, who said that to receive a little grace, one has first to make oneself empty.

Calaferte: Simone Weil wrote an amazing sentence, one that is metaphysically among the most extraordinary I know: "To believe in God does not rest with us." When you have understood that, you have understood a great many things. If I get down on my knees, it's that I have already been authorized to kneel. It's that I am already in harmony with certain zones that are zones of the cosmos, of the totality of the whole, zones that will be forces for me. Here Simone Weil has tapped into something prodigious.

Pauty: The church, the ecclesiastic institutions, excluded Simone Weil—and also Teilhard de Chardin, although he was one of their own.

Calaferte: And Galileo . . . They ban all truth!

Pauty: The theories of Teilhard de Chardin, his "astral body" idea, did all that ever interest you?

Calaferte: I was very drawn to esoterism at a certain moment but never to its forms of observance, which interest me much less than its spirit. It has been said symbolically that "man does not live by bread alone," meaning that we are something else than forms, than bodies. If we were only forms, man could not bear himself, even at the lowest level of intellectuality. He can bear himself only because he thinks, because he senses himself and senses others. These are states, formulations, that immediately go beyond mere corporality. As a solely corporal being, man does not accept himself.

Social structures such as prisons, internment, would not even be conceivable if one did not know that, in these very particular cases, man immediately or almost immediately loses his corporality to become spirit. A man whom you imprison becomes a power. It is incomprehensible that governments should ignore this. A man deprived of freedom is a power.

incarnation
....

Jean-Pierre Pauty: The titles of your books all have precise meanings, they reflect or point in the direction of your thought, for example: *Le Chemin de Sion* [*The Road to Zion*], *L'Or et le Plomb* [*Gold and Lead*], *Memento mori, Le Spectateur immobile* [*The Motionless Spectator*]; but why *L'Incarnation* [*Incarnation*], this Christian dogma signifying God's physical incarnation in the flesh of Christ, when your book is about the dark impulses of the child and the adult?

Louis Calaferte: I am being "incarnated." I am small and I am being incarnated. I am going to become a man if possible and I am being incarnated.

As far as my titles go, I try as much as possible to give the eye, the person who sees, a spiritualist notion of the world; even when the subject is a person's impulses, his purely carnal discoveries.

Pauty: The large piece of red rag, the "chi," as you describe it in your book, this silky cloth that the child perpetually drags about with him, rolls up inside of, is that all the solitude of childhood? Is it the only thing he has left in order not to be alone in the world?

Calaferte: It's personal. I can't give an interpretation; it's entirely personal. The "chi" has to do with the birth of sensuality in the child, or somewhat more than sensuality, with the birth of sexuality. It shows a need for possession—a loose possession, since the "chi" offers no resistance. If we were to venture into psychoanalytic interpretations, you might see in it the desire to possess a woman or some such twaddle.

Pauty: You have told me that you never read Lou Andreas Salome's *L'Amour du narcissisme.*

Calaferte: No, but you have spoken to me about it.

Pauty: The book deals with the same problems that you describe: the anal and the sexual. . . .

Calaferte: Anal, not really for me, but sexual, certainly! It's true that the first possible form of sexuality is sucking. The "chi" is also an image of femininity in its aspect as fabric, cloth, rustling, but that of course is a later analysis; the child, for his part, is just happy to suck on his bit of cloth. Yet the child is aware, and when I say the child I mean myself. I then am distinctly aware of doing something reprehensible. And I don't know why.

The "chi" is associated in my mind with a flood of images that are images of purely sexual exploration, a behavior that took shape early on in me, though mine is surely not an unusual case. Or was it my memory that began functioning at an early age?

I have very precocious images of my first sexual behavior, not just sensual but truly sexual. I have some external points of reference that are well established, very reliable, and altogether certain. From the age of four, I was frantically seeking women, frantically seeking physical pleasure, of that I was perfectly aware. I didn't know what it all meant, but I was aware of it.

Pauty: Freud was among the first to talk of the sexual impulses of children, something which is still not entirely accepted, since you have told me you received letters full of insults from psychologists when *L'Incarnation* was published.

Calaferte: This is another instance of Catholic oppression, and not just Catholic but oppression on the part of organized religions generally. Anything sexual is prohibited, even today when we purport to be living in a time of liberated morals. It isn't true. In our families we are still hiding our faces when the little boy show us his erect "weewee." In France, a girl who "fucks" at the age of fifteen is a slut. Everyone knows this! If she "fucks" at sixty she's lecherous. You have to apply for a permit at the town hall to find out when it's permissible.

Pauty: What did these psychologists reproach you for? Not explaining enough? Or not commenting enough? For inventing things?

Calaferte: No, not that I invented things but that I attached "too great importance to unconscious attitudes." In my own case it was anything but unconscious! I was as conscious as they come! I was on all fours on the floor trying to get a look at the legs and thighs of women, at a time when they wore relatively long dresses. I was on the prowl, I would wriggle along the floor, taking advantage of the fact that I was low to the ground and that no one was paying any attention to me, fascinated by the carnal attraction of women. I was entirely conscious!

Pauty: In short, you are reproached for talking about what is never talked about, for saying loud and clear that childhood sexuality exists.

Calaferte: I think there are thousands of cute chubby-cheeked little babies who are all doing exactly the same thing. They may not remember it very clearly, that's possible. In my case, as I've just said, there are material points of reference that I can date to when I was about four. Beginning then, woman seemed a mystery to me, the elusive source of a troubling emotion. Was it owing to my small size in relation to their tall legs rising above me? To invisibility? Under a woman's dress, when you are on the ground, you don't see much. You discern. You see vaguely. You interpret. You glimpse a shadow. All of this has stayed with me.

Today still, women are a mystery to me. I know perfectly well that when I undress a woman I am not going to discover an alarm clock, but her drawing near is still a psychological mystery that disconcerts me psychically toward her and justifies a sexual quest. The two are linked for me.

Pauty: In your descriptions, in everything that bears upon childhood, one can sense an affective void, the quest for something. Don't you think that sex was a kind of compensation for everything else?

Calaferte: I honestly don't know.

Pauty: Evoking your childhood, you often speak of the feeling of abandonment, of loneliness. . . .

Calaferte: It's a feeling that has never left me. . . .

Pauty: Here you are in agreement with the psychoanalysts: certain childhood traumas stay with you all your life. You were saying you didn't want to return to your childhood in your writing, yet you returned to it in *L'Incarnation.*

Calaferte: I don't want to gainsay the psychoanalysts all the time, there is no point in that. I think that in every respect my childhood was a bit on the rocky side.

Pauty: "Show me a child of six, and I'll tell you who he will become"?

Calaferte: Even before then. Long before, in my opinion. A child's physical behavior, the question of the nearness of bodies, of the pressure of bodies, the question of sucking, of anger, of temper tantrums, which are simply fits of jealousy. Right there, in potential form, you have the definition of an individual as he will grow up to be later on. That's why one has got to be very careful, but be careful how? Here also I think that destiny shapes itself in a certain direction and not in others.

the way it works with women

....

Jean-Pierre Pauty: A reader might draw a parallel between *The Way It Works with Women* and the end of *Septentrion:* sex as the initiatory path toward spiritual and intellectual rebirth. But unlike *Septentrion,* where you give very specific philosophical and mystical references, in *The Way It Works with Women* you provide no key. Are you only describing what you have heard, what you have seen?

Louis Calaferte: Yes, that was deliberate. The book is a report. At the same time, it's an admission through my intermediary.

I think it was an important clarification, a necessary and indispensable airing. Why this kind of concealment that weighs upon the problem of sex? Once again, the problem is of a religious nature. There would be no problem of sex if it weren't for the churches! I'm sorry but it is not men who invented the problem of sex, it's the churches! The men of the church!

Pauty: You say all the same that the erotic is man's problematic part.

Calaferte: Eroticism is something else. It's a very agreeable play of the mind, generally aesthetic, if you find anything your aesthetic sense can take hold of. Eroticism is an initiatory path, not toward possession but toward a sort of discovery of what the other may convey—and which you can never know better than through the erotic. It's the moment when you know it best, when it discloses itself most truthfully, and most of the time unconsciously. When the eroticism is conscious, there intervenes a kind of theatricality that I no longer find interesting.

The unconscious aspect of the erotic is something that deserves thought. There we are in the deepest reaches of an individual's sensibility. This is also a realm that is kept concealed, yet one that should be taken account of, as it involves an ultra-delicate form of life that shuns burdensome contingencies. In some way, this is where, for me, sex joins with spirituality, with spiritualism. We attain conjointly, from one person to another, those zones that are the most elusive of all, the most sensitive, the most precious. These games of the mind cannot be renewed often with a given individual, inasmuch as theatricality intervenes in the wake of habit.

Pauty: When *The Way It Works with Women* was published, there were some who reproached you, oddly enough, with having invented the utterances you ascribed to women. Critics said that these were your personal fantasies, that women don't have fantasies of this sort.

Calaferte: I'd like to say once again that I have very little imagination. I don't invent anything at all. I write my life, my experiences, my personal knowledge, however little I have. Only the true interests me. It's not that I'm insensitive to the imaginary, but I prefer it in others than in myself. My own imaginative life is faint, practically nonexistent. What arrests me is the true, and the why of the true. With *The Way It Works with Women* I got, strangely enough, incredible protests from men. I thought they would come from women, but not at all. Toward this book women had a simpler attitude—they had the honesty to recognize themselves in it. Among the men, there was again the same repression of sexual impulses that makes it hard for them to admit that there can exist powerful erotic games that go beyond the ordinary terms of an immediate sexuality.

Eroticism is a form of intellectualism. For the idiot there can be no eroticism, it's ruled out.

Pauty: You say that sex is connected up to the thinking mind. If man forgets that, sex can become a pointless corporal obsession.

Calaferte: You blow your nose twice or three times a day when you have a cold, and no one takes any notice of it. . . .

If the mental, cerebral universe is not connected to the sexual universe, it results in no more than copulation on the level of simple animal copulation dedicated to reproduction. Which surely has its necessity too.

Pauty: Julien Green says that the quest for the erotic leads to murder and death.

Calaferte: Poor Julien Green! His thinking is the direct offshoot of an American Protestantism transplanted in France, and I believe he has never really resolved the problem of his own sexuality. To date he has filled three thousand pages of diary without ever touching on anything that concerns him sexually. Unbelievable, don't you agree? We are told that there will be fabulous revelations after his death. Maybe. I'll be dead before that happens!

Eroticism is a game, it is the highest excellence of intellectuality in a realm called sexuality. Eroticism leads nowhere but to eroticism, that is, to the fulfillment of a refined and inventive part of the individual, and also to links with the other, to a knowledge of what the world might be, of "the mechanics of the world." There's the way it works with women. There is also the way it works with the world!

Pauty: You have been criticized for the implication of the title *The Way It Works with Women.* Is there only one way?

Calaferte: No. I could have called it "The Way It Works with Certain Women," or "One Way it Works." In any case the sexual and erotic workings of the title are described in what strikes me as a fairly general way. I don't go into particular perversions, that belongs to a different register.

Pauty: You have been interested in certain women—the Hecate type. How has it happened that you have not examined the myth of Pandora: beauty as a trap for men who take themselves for God?

Calaferte: All beauty is a trap, there is no doubt about it! All beauty is a trap, because all beauty eludes one's grasp. I forget which writer it was who, in one of his stories, cut up and embalmed faces in order to have them eternally present in all their youthfulness—they faded of course. Being an elusive entity, beauty becomes an irritant, both beauty and what beauty gives forth. Likewise the sensuality given forth by a woman's bearing. Beauty is in itself exasperating because it is inexplicable.

Lots of people over the centuries have tried to define the canons of beauty, but it always comes down to the same problem, the problem of elusiveness. Beauty remains disconcerting and troubling. What is strange and strikes me often is that when we talk of beauty, we mean woman. It's strange, because in fact women do not really seek out beauty, they are not really taken with this notion of beauty in man. Beauty is so incomprehensible, so violent, that frequently men are frightened by it. Yes, beauty is frightening.

Pauty: For Georges Bataille, the more beautiful a woman was, the greater the need to defile her, the more a man wanted to abase her. "The point is to desecrate that face, its beauty." [1]

Calaferte: That is the side I don't like in Bataille. On the contrary, beauty inspires me with the idea of exalting it, divinizing it, even venerating it. I am perfectly prepared to worship beauty, to fall every day under its enchantment. Not at all to attempt to abase it.

In no way do I support the idea of abasement with regard to man, and Bataille falls, alas, into the trap set by organized religion—we know his background. He drags us into the system of exorcism! For my part, I have nothing to exorcize! The world has nothing to exorcize. Beauty exists, and it must be accepted for what it is. It must be accepted as a gift of heaven.

Beauty may also be satanic and demonic, that is true. It is one of the forces of satanic seduction. But foremost it is charm—not in the esoteric sense but in the immediate sense.

Pauty: Another point of difference with Bataille has to do with inner experience. While for you it opens onto transcendence and faith, for him it opens onto nothingness, a *"summa atheologica."*

Calaferte: I have trouble understanding how a man like Bataille, capable of creating the body of work that he did, could arrive at a kind of fundamental negation. There is something missing there. It isn't subject to discussion. It's his way of proceeding, he has explained it to us, but I don't find it convincing;

to be sure, if I had explained my way of proceeding to him, it would probably not have convinced him either.

Pauty: What is paradoxical in Bataille is that pleasure, taken in violation of the forbidden, establishes God's absence. When Madame Edwarda comes to orgasm in the taxi, a voice mockingly asks her: "So where is your God now?" In your opinion does pleasure prove the absence of God?

Calaferte: Pleasure proves the existence of God. Pleasure is God.

I start from the principle that everything is God or nothing is God. If nothing is God, then nothing is God. If everything is God, then pleasure is God. And since for me everything is God, pleasure is God.

If one speaks clinically of what pleasure is at its extreme point of violence, it is, after all, a breaking through, like it or not, a sudden bursting out onto some transcending thing. And this thing, this transcendence, if you don't care to call it God you can call it peanut, but in any case it's the transcendence that accompanies peanut. I am taken aback by Bataille's kind of reasoning. I fear it's a sign of impotence, but I don't want to pass judgment, as I have no proof.

Pauty: Bataille raised transgression and the forbidden to the level of concepts. Is pleasure merely a matter of the forbidden?

Calaferte: In my cosmogony, there is no prohibition. The only thing forbidden is the harming of others. If I harm you, I disturb some element of you, I become responsible for disturbing the harmony that was yours. I am the cause of something defective. This renders me responsible, I enter into the category of the destructive.

Pauty: Do you posit the suffering of others as the limit beyond which one must not go in search of one's own pleasure?

Calaferte: Suffering is Evil. It is not God. God is that which is life. Death is still part of life. The ninety-nine percent conscious practice of Evil is Evil, it is not God.

Everything that is happiness, pleasure, seduction, love, woman, reading, tree, desire, lust, that is God! I have said so in my writing: a flower is God, a woman's smile, a fine face, this is God. The female guards at Bergen-Belsen I mentioned earlier, that's the devil! It's plain to see! You just have to look and you know that it's the devil.

Now, you have to know what your glance has fallen on. You can also amuse yourself by looking at the devil. Why not? That's not forbidden either. You just have to know at what point you'll be able to stop and not go too far. Today, in Paris and elsewhere, there are large demonic sects that are extremely effective and efficient. I believe that this indicates a loss of life. Today, man is afraid of living. If you are afraid of death, then you are afraid of living! Death is a force.

Pauty: And suffering?

Calaferte: Suffering is another problem. Who is innocent? The question has to be asked. Who is innocent?

Pauty: For you *The Way It Works with Women* should be thought of as a metaphysical approach to the world, yet the book has wound up on the shelves of porn shops, like Henry Miller's *Sexus* only a few years ago. Doesn't this suggest a misunderstanding?

Calaferte: A total misunderstanding! The book sells very well, but the people who buy it are not my real readers, they are a different set of people. You just have to hope that two or three among them will stay on for the next book.

Pauty: This brings us to the problem of the different levels of reading, of interpretation, that your work gives rise to. Some see nothing in your writing but sex, darkness, and violence and are unaware of the believer, the man of ideas, the rebel. Yet on your side, you speak of unity. The level at which your work is read, it seems to me, is closely tied to the personality of the reader. The philosopher Paul Ricoeur says that a universal and identical decoding is impossible. Is this where the misunderstanding arises?

Calaferte: There is an appalling lack of curiosity in France, a curiosity I know something about since my work is very diverse. I wanted it that way—I loathe repetition—being interested in a thousand things. And I believe that to be interested in a thousand things is to go in the direction of life.

I have one category of faithful readers who have read my books but never read a line of my plays! And I also have the reverse, people who ritually come to see my plays performed but who have never read a line of my writing. It surprises me. It's true that my theater is a theater of derision, a comic theater that can be disconcerting but that carries no sense of an underlying worsening of our situation, a concept common to all my books. Those theatergoers don't accept me in totality. Now, ought they to accept me? I don't know, it's not for me to decide. But it's true that in this there is a bit of distortion.

Pauty: Such taking into account of the complexity, of the totality of a writer's oeuvre has never really been accepted practice. This meant all sorts of difficulties for such artists as Leonardo da Vinci and Pico della Mirandola, whose multitude of interests

On the set of the film *Un îlot de résistance*. Preparation for the sequence on painting.
Right, director Jean-Pierre Pauty. Paris, 1993. (Photograph, N.M.)

led them to explore many paths. Has nothing changed in the twentieth century?

Calaferte: No. Nothing has changed, you're right. Everything and everyone is given a label.

Pauty: You have to confine yourself to your domain.

Calaferte: My offhanded attitude toward this social norm has been detrimental to me, I know that.

If tomorrow I go and write about airplanes, people will say "Now what's he poking his nose into!" But if airplanes are what interest me, why shouldn't I?

With painting it's the same thing. I've always painted, ever since I was sixteen or eighteen, and I've always kept this activity in a corner. I don't think of myself as a painter, let's not exaggerate, but I have all the same accumulated a rather considerable body of pictorial work, perhaps five thousand pieces, counting objects and drawings. Well, among those who like me for my literary activity, practically no one has shown interest in my painting. The diversity of my work puts people off. I become a jack-of-all-trades, with all the pejorative associations that has for the French mind—someone who doesn't deal seriously with anything. In actual fact I do deal with things seriously, even when I paint.

Pauty: Your interest in painting is one of the points you have in common with Henry Miller. He drew on "other interior designs" when he painted.

Calaferte: Henry Miller's work is poorly known, for all his wide reputation. There is a great deal to say about him, to interpret. Miller has suffered from that. He is still undiscovered. He is a very great writer because he is a "man of life." He arrives here, he adores Europe, he adores France, the sources of civilization, Greece. His attitude is nonetheless American, in that it is fundamentally drawn to freedom, whereas our minds are fundamentally shriveled. The freedom of his work has played a great part in his success, a success that I believe is founded on misunderstanding. Miller is a serious author. He is a philosopher. I hold him to be, along with Proust and Joyce (though for other reasons), among the four or five greats of this century. They are the beacons of this century.

Miller is one of the beacons of this century and not, I repeat, for his contributions of sex and violence, that has little interest, because again it's poorly understood. That's not what Miller is about.

Pauty: There was a time when *Sexus* was found mainly in porn shops!

Calaferte: How idiotic! Miller is to be read by thoughtful, attentive, intelligent people who ask themselves serious questions about the world. Miller provides no ready answers, but he asks questions with an enormous sincerity and an enormous love of life.

Pauty: His spirituality was evident: "A true artist directs the reader back to himself, helps him to discover in himself the inexhaustible riches he possesses. No one can be saved or cured other than through his own efforts. The only remedy is faith."

Calaferte: Yes. And there are a great many other passages you could quote. Miller has been a victim of success, of scandal.

Pauty: With the effect of "reducing" him, reducing his thought?

Calaferte: That's right. They all see eye to eye when it comes to that. The publishers themselves, who profit from a book's success. The cash-drawer publishers. You're dreaming if you think there are publishers who are amateurs of art, I certainly don't know any. I'm waiting to be introduced to one.

There is such a thing as willfully reducing someone. I know what I'm talking about. In my case, as with Miller, they went so far as to ban my book, *Septentrion*. They are so dumb they only have one refuge: direct censorship! A printed book, even if it exists in only three copies, continues to circulate around the world. A book should never be banned. These are Nazi autos-da-fé. However you burn it, there will always be one left! The stupidity, the helplessness are beyond belief!

Pauty: By way of promoting scandal to sells books, there have recently been headlines about "Miller an anti-Semite," with no mention anywhere of his real position—which has always been perfectly clear and unambiguous.[2]

Calaferte: How can anyone attribute such thinking to Henry Miller! Miller is so in love with man, has such a feeling for life, that the idea of anti-Semitism—and the same holds for me— could never germinate in him. To be an anti-Semite you have to be a jerk, above all else! So long as you're not a jerk, so long as you're a thinking person, there isn't any "Jewish question," as it's so nicely put. There's only the question of jerkishness, which is a whole different thing! Once the question of jerkishness is taken care of, then the question of anti-Semitism and racism generally will have been taken care of too. It is a narrowing, a shrinking, the anti-Semitic idea. You find it in the middle classes, and in the subproletarian classes, so preoccupied with the notion of the power possessed by the other players: he has taken everything from us, therefore he must be got rid of, that way we'll have it all. That's the subproletariat's impoverished thinking, which I've experienced, which I've known, whose component forces are thoroughly familiar to me, and which obviously can be very dangerous, though not unless it receives help from the outside. There has to be an anti-Semitic mechanism working at a higher level to steer it, because the anti-Semitism of the subproletariat is powerless on its own.

Pauty: Another notable difference that I'd like to point out, and one that separates you from Georges Bataille, an enthusiast of bullfighting, is the evidence you've given in the *Carnets* over the past thirty years of your respect and love for animals.

Calaferte: It's not just a love of animals, it's a love of life! Of all that is alive. From the ant to the butterfly. The only people who watch spectacles like bullfights are the impotent! I'll stick to it—they have a sexual problem somewhere: either they go to bullfights to get a hard-on and have a good fuck afterward, or else they never get a hard-on and never fuck, which is also possible. I have been told by people, by people in the business and who hang around these kinds of spectacles, that in Spain there is no end of whorehouses in the vicinity of the bullring! How such people as Hemingway, Montherlant, or, I'm sorry to say, Picasso can have enjoyed such barbarous shows, especially when Picasso was Jewish, is inconceivable to me. I don't know the nature of Picasso's sexuality, his women never told, which is a shame, but there is no paradox; I seriously believe that any individual with a relation of cruelty toward other living beings has a problem of sexuality.

the sands of time

....

Jean-Pierre Pauty: Among the books you have written, *Les Sables du temps* is one of your personal favorites. In it you address several domains: dreams, astrology, your own existence, and artistic creation. In connection with the last, you say something disturbing: that in the midst of a period of creation the artist is as if situated outside of time and inside a kind of magic circle where nothing can happen to him.

Louis Calaferte: And nothing does happen to him. What I say there is an empirical statement! I never speak of anything except from experience. The moment you are in that state of grace called the state of creation, the world around you stops. You're in a state of force that supplants it. The mechanical, or rather, the organic progression of the world, this progression of social developments we are confronted with, is miraculously suspended while the period of creation lasts. Such is the tension that it brings about a modification of the "existential planes," and you benefit from this extraordinary modification. Unfortunately the magic only lasts as long as the creative tension does. The moment it ceases—and in my case it ceases rather quickly, which is why I write very, very fast—sometimes, amazingly enough, the very day, the very moment you finish a book, you come to a stop without knowing whether the book is finished or not but you sense that the inspiration is drying up, and immediately some problem crops up . . . as if the external world had been lying in wait. Before, nothing could get through. There was a magic circle, nothing could come in. When the period of creativity is over, the sluices open. After the writing of some of my books, not of all of them, but several, I was suddenly faced with an accumulation of problems, a sudden onslaught from the outside.

A sort of miracle occurs. I believe works of art are truly sacred, and that we are not authorized to make disparaging judgments on what is art, which is to say, something absolutely authentic on the part of a human being. Again, I say this without the least trace of personal vanity.

Pauty: During love, in certain cases, we may likewise feel ourselves to be outside of time.

Calaferte: It's of the same order. With the difference that the creative act is going to extend in continuous fashion over a month, over two months, permanently, continually, day after day, which, you'll agree, is not always the case with sexuality. Something entirely magical happens. I know that in the eyes of some it appears to be fabrications, ephemera created by the mind.

Pauty: In which case, Gérard de Nerval, Robert Louis Stevenson, Swedenborg, André Breton, André Hardellet, etc., should no longer exist.

Calaferte: I stand by this because I have experienced it. Though my health is extremely deficient, I am never sick while I write. As soon as it's finished, a change occurs.

Pauty: Jung says that in a work of art there are things beyond the artist's will, resurgences of the millennial soul that reappear in the form of eternal symbols.

Calaferte: I am entirely of the same opinion. For me, art is a "gift." It is given to you. By whom I have no idea. I have written some sixty books, and sometimes my wife will read me excerpts from them that appear in newspapers or journals, and I'll have no recollection of them at all. I totally forget what I have written, to the point of not even knowing that I am the author of this or that, which amuses us a great deal. I could never remake what I have made already. Truly, I wouldn't be able to. I tell myself I am a worker who "makes." When Jung mentions the collective unconscious as the source of all works of art, I agree completely. I don't know how he approached the matter, but it's entirely true. Otherwise you have fabrications. Most of the time we are dealing with people who calculate, who tell themselves before they start writing that such and such will occur on page two, on page three. To me that's inconceivable. Absolutely inconceivable.

Pauty: You have to be sincere.

Calaferte: Yes, otherwise nothing happens. That's why a book becomes difficult to the extent that it is sincere, that it is given. No, it's not even a question of sincerity or insincerity—

Pauty: I was using sincere in the sense that you don't cheat in your dealings with yourself, you don't conceal anything.

Calaferte: You can't cheat. I don't know whether later, when we part, I will sit down and write something. I just don't know. In this very hotel room, the one we are in now, on this little table, last February 18, after a brief conversation with my wife, I started *C'est la guerre*. Twenty-one days later I had finished it. The book is two hundred pages long.

The form is given to you. I am not an inventor of forms.

Pauty: That's what Paul Valéry said, "The first verse is given to you."

Calaferte: Yes, and the others are not always very good. One should only write down first verses! The others, you look for them. . . .

Poetry is a strange realm. You're in a completely different state from the one governing the writing of a book. It's a type of nostalgic state where you're having to do with you're not quite sure what. In addition, you don't feel very well, you don't know what you want to say; then a first verse is given to you which is generally rather beautiful. After that, it all relies on your execution!

Pauty: When Rimbaud presented his great poem "The Drunken Boat" to the literary lights of his day, he was advised to alter the first verse and remove the "as" of "As I floated down impassive rivers" and to begin with "I am a boat that. . . ."

Calaferte: It's the old struggle between creators and fabricators. About two months ago I met some of these fabricators, famous ones, and I was stunned. I can assure you that creation is the least of their concerns. Only one thing interested them, fabricating books and selling them. They are not creators, they are tinkers.

Pauty: Can you remember a book in which, after it was done, you discovered things you hadn't thought of while writing it?

Calaferte: I receive lots of mail. I have had three experiences.

Louis Calaferte. Bordeaux, 1987. (Photograph, Louis Monier)

A woman wrote me: "I'm going to die, I have cancer, I have one of your *Carnets* on my bedside table, thank you for writing it." People don't talk lightly when they are on the brink of passing. Another woman came up to me in a bookstore, took my hand, and said: "Thank you for my son. He died. Thank you on his behalf." In the same circumstances, in Lyons, an old woman also took my hands and murmured: "A special grace hangs over you." That happens, and you can't think what it was you wrote.

Pauty: It must have been gratifying. For once you weren't the "devil."

Calaferte: Yes and no. . . . This sort of testimonial embarrasses me because I look upon myself as a simple executor. Whether it's by Louis Calaferte or Mr. X has no importance, I insist on this point, I'm not vain in that way. It's only that I am thankful to be able to "make" things, since in a case like that I feel happy.

Pauty: On one side are the people who find you harmful and extremist, who condemn your violence and ban *Septentrion;* and on the other are those who write thanking you for the moral and spiritual comfort they have found from reading your *Carnets.* One can gauge here the subjectivity of the judges and critics who decide what is good or not good for others.

Calaferte: All I can say is, I don't appeal to people who are lukewarm—because anyone who says "a special grace hangs over you" is already excessive in her own right! We are in regions where almost magical forces rule. I am a halfway broken man at this point, yet people visit me and say: "You're in such great shape!" I'm not in any kind of shape. No, not in any kind. I greet life, that's all. And the work is life, provided you set the highest standards!

Pauty: Let's talk for a moment about this matter of the work and the life of the artist in connection with what he writes. Artists often reproach churchmen and politicians with not incarnating their own fine words, but doesn't the artist also have some responsibilities in this area?

Calaferte: Yes . . . yes. . . .

Pauty: I say this because you have written that "Words make everything tremble." But if the reader knows that the artist who has written these words does not incarnate them, why would he take him more seriously than a politician or a clergyman? In this way despair takes root, nothing is sacred any longer, nothing merits one's faith.

Calaferte: There's a question here of vocabulary, of terminology. Are you saying "artist" or "pseudoartist"? If you're saying "artist," the artist is irreproachable. According to Joyce: "Genius is always right." There are people who claim to be artists and are not. If you are an artist, you live as an artist, it follows inevitably. You don't dream of bank accounts, you are not going to have a yacht on the Mediterranean, you won't own a Rolls Royce, and so on. I have always lived without a car, in my life I have had one motorcycle—even then it wasn't I who bought it.

Pauty: You don't accept the schizophrenic separation that some people make: on this side is my life, on the other my work.

Calaferte: No . . . no. . . . There is what I was made for and what I have done that coheres with what I was made for. As to its value, that's another question. What I have done may be of no value at all, I have no idea, time will tell. If I die tomorrow morning, by the following day my work may have dropped out of sight, it's altogether possible, but I know that I was made to do that work, so I did it and doing it has occupied my entire life, it occupies my mind all the time, truly! Sometimes I walk in my garden and I talk to the flowers, the plants, and I tell myself that I am fortunate to be able to talk to the flowers, but it is not something I ever worked toward, it's the way I am.

I don't believe you can differentiate the work from the man, but with certain artists, it has to be said, there are also "gray areas." I don't think I have any truly dangerous gray areas.

Pauty: Areas that would cause your writings to be seen as an imposture?

Calaferte: I don't know, I don't think so. When I speak about gray areas, I think of Céline, who is inarguably an artist, inarguably a literary force, yet who goes out and commits murder—because it is tantamount to murder—literary murder, by publishing his pamphlets *Bagatelles pour un massacre,* and the rest.

Pauty: Céline says horrible things: "Men need hatred in order to live, agreed! . . . Let them have it for Jews, this hatred of theirs, not for Germans."[1] "I would prefer twelve Hitlers to one all-powerful [Léon Blum]," and "If in the Great Adventure sacrificial calves are needed, then let the Jews be bled! That's my opinion!"[2] It's vile.

Calaferte: Yes, it's vile. It is very curious that French intellectuals are able to think their way into such heresies, such unimaginable heresies. Maurice Barrès, an anti-Dreyfusard and a literary nullity who, until 1930 or 1935, held an important place in French letters, declared, when Dreyfus was convicted and deported to Devil's Island where the temperatures are 120 degrees in the shade: "It's a good thing, it will serinate him!"[3] It's horrible to make up the word "serinate" in order to say that this man is going to be made sick from heat and sunstroke. Unfortunately, you find that pretty often in French literature, you find it in a man like Léon Bloy.

Pauty: To whom you have been compared.

Calaferte: I would hate for there to be the slightest confusion. Bloy was not a charitable man. He lived the life of a martyr, he endured it—to do so requires qualities—in the name of his genius, but he was not a charitable man, he was a hard man. He reminds me all too often of an ecclesiastic. He is rather close in condition to a cardinal, to one of those people whose head is Christian and whose heart is in hell. His case seems to me like that. I don't like the guy. I have a fair number of comments on him in my *Carnets,* because I often pick up and reread his diary. He has many seductive aspects. He is also a forthright man, he doesn't hide his hatreds, his antipathies. I think there is a primary side to him that would have benefited from listening to the voice of reason. I am sorry he had his failings, just as I am with Céline. In Céline's case, I don't know enough about his life, his private life. The hatred that he stored up, where did it come from? How did it arise? That's what seems a little strange to me. With him too there is something missing. I am not far from believing that here again we see the consequence of a sexual problem.

Pauty: One of his painter friends, who had known him since childhood, said that Céline had grown up with anti-Semitism all around him, in a neighborhood where it was a common thing.

Calaferte: I come from the same sort of neighborhoods as Céline, the slums. I am not an anti-Semite.

Pauty: Yes, but you were a "wop," you were an immigrant, a foreigner. You were subject to racism yourself, as were Jews, Arabs, blacks.

Calaferte: Sure. But when you're in a working-class slum, differences of race don't really exist. Origins count for very little since everyone is from somewhere else, which evens everything out. I think it's too easy to explain racism by pointing to the neighborhood a person grew up in. After all when you have the talent, the genius, of Céline you have the obligation to think a little when you have a pen in your hand. I believe that Céline is truly a criminal, and that History will continue to regard him as a criminal of talent. That's as much as you can say about him and that's all I am going to say.

Pauty: Starting with *Partage des vivants,* you were faced with the problem of the writer prostituting himself, with the problem of success, because your first book, *Requiem des innocents,* was a bestseller, and then you broke off.

Calaferte: Yes. I have broken off several times in my life.

At the outset, the problem presented itself differently. I write a book, *Requiem des innocents.* I want to become a writer. I don't know what one is. I don't know how you go about it. I bring this five- or six-hundred page manuscript to the writer Joseph Kessel, who spends a lot of time undoing and redoing this book, teaching me how to thin out a book, clear it up. From then on I was a "writer." Honestly, that was all I wanted. How innocent I was. The publisher quickly explained to me that a follow-up was needed. It was René Julliard, who, with me, behaved wonderfully, magnificently, extraordinarily. No other publisher has been so good to me. Later I found another, whose name is Gérard Bourgadier. There have been two in my life, one at the start and one at the end—there must be a sign in that. I also found an "additional" editor, Pierre Drachline, a man I hold to be an excellent and authentic writer in his own right. Three men have loved my books and fought that they might exist. After Julliard explained to me that I needed a follow-up to *Requiem,* I wrenched my gut to write that piece of trash called *Partage des vivants. Requiem* had performed wonderfully, and the follow-up did also. Julliard hoped that I would write fourteen more just like it. That's when I stopped. For five years I didn't write anything. I questioned myself for five years about my literary possibilities. I was troubled. It was a willed act, a choice. I didn't want to make a "career" of writing. For me it was something sacred, something mythic. Then I wrote *Septentrion.* It was also a settling of scores. It was banned, well, I'm not going to get off onto that again.

Pauty: On betrayal on the part of the artist, I'd like to quote this sentence by the Russian filmmaker Andrei Tarkovski: "A man who betrays his principles even once loses all purity in his relation to life. To cheat on yourself is to renounce everything, your films, your life."

Calaferte: Those are the words of a man who is an artist and who has understood the truth, the meaning of creativity. If you cheat, it's over with forever, but Tarkovski's statement is ambiguous. It gives the impression that the artist is capable of betraying himself.

I don't believe the artist can betray, betray himself; only a pseudoartist can do so. The artist is constituted in such a way that he can't betray himself, or if he does his life stops, he no longer exists and commits suicide the next day.

Pauty: Chekhov said that a falsehood pursues us all our lives.

Calaferte: Yes, that's right. I mean, that's right where an artist is concerned. It sounds very pretentious to say "an artist," let's say someone to whom God has given that function, that's what I would like to make clear.

Pauty: Tarkovski was a religious man.

Calaferte: I'm not very familiar with him. We all speak the same language. If you are an authentic artist, you're an authentic man. If you're an authentic man, you live an authentic life with respect to authenticity, not with respect to the social. In any case, the social is always reductive, and however you slice it the social is a prison.

Pauty: Blaise Pascal is one of the writers you are fond of. He wrote in "fragments," which seems more and more to be the way you are proceeding. Did he influence you?

Calaferte: No. I have had only one influence in my life and it was not Pascal. I was an ignoramus, totally without culture, a blank. So I read, I read. I don't know who has read more than I. It's frightening, the amount of reading I did. Nowadays I read less. Anyhow, there came a day when I discovered Blaise Cendrars. It was truly a revelation. I suddenly understood how a person could write. It was thanks to Cendrars that I wrote at all. I came to know him a little, but only a very little. He was terribly ill and died soon after we met.

Pauty: Yet there is no connection between your thinking and that of Cendrars?

Calaferte: No, none, but I feel eternal gratitude toward him.

The man taught me to write through his books. I didn't know him at all. I had never heard anyone pronounce his name. At a bookstore on the rue de Provence—is it still there?—I stole a book by Cendrars, I must have been eighteen years old. From that moment on I stopped reading novels, books of no interest. I understood that there were two literatures.

Pauty: Do you have any memory of your meeting with Cendrars?

Calaferte: Oh, yes! I called him up one day, I was telephoning from a metro station or a train station. He said: "Yes. . . . What do you want?" He was already old and sick; he had a tired voice. I was so embarrassed. I was extremely shy. I hung up. Nothing happened. I wrote him. He answered. I still remember his first words: "What do you want from me?" I didn't know what to reply. I finally went to see him one afternoon. He was lying down and didn't get up. He was very weak. His wife was there, but I never met his daughter. I came to know him only a very little. We saw each other two or three times and that was it. I went to his house three times, and then he died. These are memories. It all seems very far away.

Pauty: Did he give you any advice?

Calaferte: No, not at all. And I would never have dared to ask for any. I listened to him talk. I never stayed very long. He was a tired, dying man.

As to the other Blaise, Blaise Pascal, I only "met" him, encountered him, much later. I liked his madness. I liked his Jansenism, which I like a little less now. I still like his madness, but I am less fond of his condemnations. I am severe with him because they are church condemnations.

It was the wrong thing to do, to affiliate such a system as his with such a body as the church. There are things in his writing that are unacceptable, horrendous anti-Semitic passages, which are calmly published and republished because they belong to Pascal's *Pensées.*

Pauty: In the New Testament there are also problematic passages on the Jews.

Calaferte: Yes, but there it's a question of problems between the Galileans and the Jews. Occultation becomes an issue here. The Dead Sea Scrolls have not all been published, no one knows their contents, apart from a few privileged individuals.

Pauty: Given some of these texts, it is not surprising that the Jews have trouble understanding the New Testament. Shouldn't there be a return to. . . .

Calaferte: There should be a return to the human soul. To the human being. One has to situate oneself outside all these corporatisms that constrain freedom, the expansion of the individual: the body of the State, the body of the church, the body of the military. . . . When are we going to live? It is urgent and important to learn to live and to love. We must little by little succeed in imparting that.

To live, that is to be conscious of one's dignity of being.

memento mori

Jean-Pierre Pauty: In one of the texts of *Memento mori,* you have a man traveling in a train with opaque windows, and the train is moving at an infernal pace. Is that death?

Louis Calaferte: No, no. It's life, with death included. It is an initiatory vision, and its meaning is initiatory. Life is an initiation. Life is essentially an initiation. To what? To life! To death as well, probably, but still as part of life. It is true that we are entirely in that phase of life, unfortunately, but it's one of the elements of our constitution, of our being, of our function. We are traveling in a train with opaque windows. Outside are taking place things that we know about or don't know about, that we hear or don't hear, that we understand or don't understand.

We are traveling in an opaque train inside ourselves, but in traveling we move beyond ourselves. The journey is an initiatory journey, it is therefore a journey of development.

Pauty: The book ends with a sort of call into the night: "I who have venerated you to the point of sublimation, do not abandon me now." One thinks of the last words Christ spoke on the cross.

Calaferte: That parallel occurred to me, though after the fact, suggesting itself at the moment when the magic circle I spoke of earlier dissolved. I realized that I was coming to an acceptance of my own death.

Let me say straight out that several of my books have enabled me to make important advances in my own thinking, and *Memento mori* is one of those. I made a small but real leap forward with respect to my system of understanding, I did in fact define myself for myself. After writing that book I needed to integrate certain thoughts that arose, actually, from that very book, as though I were its reader and not its author. I did not, for all that, reread it—I have never reread any of my books, aside from *Septentrion,* and for very specific reasons—but the fact of having been able to write that kind of text, of having been able thus to enter a somewhat mystical realm, situated beyond the contingencies of what we call the real—which is also an imaginary construct—made me look deep into myself and probably led me onto paths that have found expression today in a book like *L'Homme vivant.*

Pauty: In *Memento mori* you mention the idea of physical suffering, which recurs, though treated from another angle, in *L'Homme vivant.* In the latter book you say that suffering is not a "punishment," that it does not prove "the death of God." The physical suffering you have endured all through your life, the persistence of the illness that recently left you almost entirely paralyzed for several months, the approach of death—these haven't shaken your faith?

Calaferte: No, not at all. Certainly I was worried, but not about my own death. I was worried about what would happen next, on a physical level. I imagined the worst, being immobilized, bedridden—that would have been the abomination of all

Louis Calaferte in conference with Guillemette on the set of the film *Un îlot de résistance*. Paris, 1993. (Photograph, N.M.)

abominations for me. But it was also a remarkable experience. Because it's easy to tell others to have faith and not to have it yourself when something dramatic happens to you. I felt myself in eternal harmony with God, and I know that I will feel that way at the moment of my passing.

I am apprehensive about pain, because I have had to endure a lot of it in my life in every respect. Especially physical pain. All right, I'm very resistant, I truly have a strong resistance to pain, but that does not prevent it from hurting a great deal, from being frightening and distressing. Yet one's transcendental powers are not affected. So there you are, paralyzed, lying in your bed, your wife has to feed you, I won't go into the rest. I'd like to pay tribute to her here, and for so much! So much! Somehow there's a body lying there and then there's me, who am something other than this body that's in pain. So I'm in pain, and that's as far as it goes.

I nonetheless wrote two collections of poems from my sickbed.

Pauty: People sometimes say "Calaferte is a hard man" or "There's no love in Calaferte." Yet all your *Carnets* pay tribute to your wife, describe unusual ties of love, tenderness, and complicity. Whence this misunderstanding? Are people once again refusing to read what's there in black and white?

Calaferte: The moment you are real, you are excessive, hard, violent. In other words, you're real!

I could have lived without love, but pitifully. The understanding that has grown up between my wife and me has been quite exceptional, coordinating my life and my work, giving suppleness to my thinking, supplementing in some way what I am. So it has been crucial.

Pauty: In his notebooks Charles de Foucauld writes: "What counts in love is not so much the love but the will to love."

Calaferte: I never really agree when people talk about the will to do this or that. Things are done because they are, because they must be.

What is incredible is the encounter. The encounter is incredible! It's dazzling and fabulous. The encounter is truly fabulous. Once the encounter has occurred, things fall into place of themselves. Life arranges itself in such sort that things can perpetuate themselves.

Pauty: Even when a fabulous chance is offered, you have to know how to make it last. There are people who destroy everything.

Calaferte: Yes, of course, especially in this domain. But that brings us back to the beginning of our interview, to our discussion about destructiveness, about the energy of the dark forces.

Pauty: If love is "given," if it is a chance, then it behooves man to understand that?

Calaferte: It behooves man to know that.

To know that, thanks to love, he is entering an extremely and exclusively privileged realm. A realm of health and sanity. When, unfortunately, you are confronted with what I call the demoniacal—my vocabulary is a bit thin but it defines what I mean well enough—when you are confronted with people who, deep down, despise love and, instead of sublimating it, act so as to lessen it, ruin it, trample it down, obliterate it, then you are dealing with people who are completely destructive. They are jackals. I class them in the category of Evil, of the demonized. It happens, I know. . . . You protect yourself, that's all you can do.

Pauty: The power of love you've been speaking of was already present in *Septentrion*. At the end of the book, for the first time in his life, the character literally goes down on his knees in front of love, in front of the woman he has just met. His entire life is transformed from that moment on. This crucial scene, this transformation of the character, this hymn to love, no one ever seems to have noticed it.

Calaferte: Yes, but what can you expect. I also told them that *La Mécanique des femmes* was a book about love. Through the erotic you attain a purity. If there is no purity, there is no eroticism.

You have to know how to read. You have to know how to hear.

You have to know how to live. Live.

an island
of resistance

On the set of *Un îlot de résistance* with Jean-Pierre Pauty. Preparation of the
sequence on childhood and the publication of *Requiem des innocents*. Paris, 1993.
(Photograph, N.M.)

Planning what we would do, Louis Calaferte and I decided that our work fell into two parts:

1. The book of interviews would concentrate particularly on his inner adventure.
2. The film would retrace his course as an artist, a rebel, and an island of resistance.[1]

"Some would have us believe that we live in the communications age! There has never been less communicated than today! Do you happen to know who the great writers of Greece, Norway, or Albania are currently? No, you don't, and if you did it would only be by accident." (See page 26.)

The public debate that occurred after his death over the failure to air this film on television was related notably in *Le Monde* (May 4, 1994) and *Le Canard enchaîné* (May 18, 1994). The arguments given for not airing it were mainly spurious; only one person "suggested" to me that I might have cut certain of Calaferte's remarks.

A short time before his death, Calaferte said to me: "I regret nothing; my life will have followed the lines laid down in my youth."

—Jean-Pierre Pauty

the theater: early days

The portion of the interview that follows, until now unpublished, was not included in the final version of the film *Un îlot de résistance* for reasons of length. Louis Calaferte was particularly concerned to evoke the person of Jean Vilar.

Jean-Pierre Pauty: In what you call the labyrinth of each existence, the Théâtre de l'Odéon has played a double role in yours.

Louis Calaferte: Yes, that theater was one of the focal points of my youth. I had quit the factory by then. I had "gone up" to Paris. Through friends I discovered the system of walk-on roles at the Odéon. It was a relatively pleasant way of life, aside from entering that world of bit players, which is a dreadful world. The walk-on is an unfortunate person who hopes not only to stop being unfortunate and unhappy but who also yearns to get ahead of those around him, insofar as he is forever hoping to be noticed, hoping to become an actor. That goes for bit-playing in the movies as well, something I also did. There it's even more dramatic.

I was seventeen, eighteen years old. One day, in a second-hand bookshop, I filched a book: one of the novels in the *Salavin* cycle by Georges Duhamel. In the opening pages,

Duhamel describes Paris as one of the coldest places in the world, and in my state of destitution, of desolation, of total powerlessness during the unusually severe winter of 1946, that was in fact my experience.

Then I became a writer.

Later I had the pleasure of seeing my first play produced at the Odéon Theater, directed by Jean-Pierre Miquel and with a cast of remarkable actors. That play, *Chez les Titch,* turned out to be in harmony with the spirit of its audience and did very nicely.

Compared to the pretty dreadful feeling of perdition that accompanied my youth, when I had no idea where I was going, envisaging the worst, waking to despair just about every morning without anything to eat, I have to say—all vanity aside—that for me it was a kind of little revenge. There again you want to give thanks to that something which directs your footsteps. There, in a nutshell, is my little "adventure."

Pauty: You have told me that during this difficult period of your youth you came across a remarkable person.

Calaferte: Yes, I met a number of unusual persons when I was an extra, and there was one in particular, whom I came across in the loge of a patron of the Grand Odéon where many people used to come and go.

One night, the door of this sumptuous loge opened to reveal a rather strange-looking gentleman, in a state of awful poverty. He had on a long overcoat, which seemed to be hiding an absence of clothing underneath, and, with his stove-in hat, the effect was right out of an American movie of the 1930s.

In impassioned terms he stigmatized everyone there, trying to enlist these very official actors in the crazy adventure of a great itinerant theater of the people. He got no response

Louis Calaferte. Chevigny, 1975. (Photograph, collection G. Calaferte)

whatever, not even of sympathy. I was greatly affected by this, as our conditions of existence seemed pretty much alike; I was in about the same straits as he, so anomalous in this ultraluxurious loge. This man was struggling in a desert.

From my corner, I observed this personage. Unforgettable features: a gaunt, emaciated face. Someone at once very determined and rather ground down by life.

Then one thing particularly drew me to him: a tiny insect, a flea, was making its way up and down the collar of the big overcoat that covered everything real and imagined. Everyone was looking at him with condescension and alarm, wondering when this chinch bug would leave. That man was Jean Vilar.

Pauty: Jean Vilar, who a few years later was to found the Avignon Theater Festival and the Théâtre National Populaire.

Calaferte: I was struck by this scene, by this image of official, conventional success, which was also an image of spiritual poverty, face-to-face with the violent desire of a man who wanted to practice an authentic art.

On that day there were present within a very small space both of these two types of men that one continues to encounter in this profession all one's life.

Pauty: Actors and the theater have played an important role in your life, since it was an actor who encouraged you to write for the theater.

Calaferte: It's someone I would like to pay tribute to, Monsieur Guy Rapp, an actor and director in the years 1948 to 1949. He was a true man of the theater, a person of great sincerity. That man spurred me to write a hundred pages of dialogues.

Pauty: Living in a working-class neighborhood, working in a factory at the age of thirteen, you write in your *Carnets* that at this time you became interested in Shakespeare. How was that ever possible?

Calaferte: It was entirely accidental, books being a possession unknown in my milieu and among my familiars. I stole a Shakespeare, at random—there was no way in my financial situation that I could buy even a single book—and it could just as well have been Cervantes or another.

What fascinated me in Shakespeare was the lyricism, the "beyondness," an extraordinary magma in which men and women were loving each other passionately, killing each other passionately; a fascination owing also to the presence of gravediggers.

Pauty: Do you remember which was your first Shakespeare play?

Calaferte: No, I can't remember.

Pauty: It must have been *Hamlet* with its great gravedigger scene. Strange coincidence for someone who would build his work around the existential question, the question of "to be."

Calaferte: Frankly, I hadn't reached that stage yet. I was just excited that there were gravediggers. . . . After that, I started writing things that weren't worth much but that reflected the great lyricism that was already part of my nature and that is part of me to this day.

intimist theater and baroque theater

There are two strains in my plays: intimist theater and baroque theater.

My plays contain a comic element that is strong, clear, and intended; but at the same time this comic element is a comedy of derision. It's a comedy of observation.

Poverty and death, for example, are comical—tragic as that may be—because they lie outside the normal sphere. That poverty and death should actually be horrific, unacceptable, unbearable, that is another issue.

I'd call it a nostalgia for derision, because derision is not only critical and vindictive but a form of despair. That's what I tried to capture in my intimist plays.

I feel that I am close, relatively speaking, to a man like Chekhov and also to a ragged, woeful madness like Strindberg's.

There came a point when it seemed that I was through with derision, the narrow, enclosed, almost familial derision of what I call my intimist plays.

In the other kind of plays I have written, the ones I call baroque, the derision has been joined by an anarchizing element that is very important to me.

These plays have had more difficulty finding an audience than the others. The intimist plays, for their part, touch people to the quick but don't disturb them politically.

I believe in the real, in experience, in observation, which is to say the relation of the real to experience.

Whether I am writing prose or plays, my goal is always the same: to express experienced reality. Not a theoretical reality. I never move out of the autobiographical frame.

Creation is life. As soon as you are no longer making life, you are no longer a creator.

Art is a desire to be, a desire to live.

During the shooting of the film *Un îlot de résistance*. Paris, July 24, 1993. (Photograph, N.M.)

painting

Painting, with me, is simply the expression of a poetic necessity.

A painting is not only an image but a sign. It is made less to be looked at than to be thought about. Once completed, the painting implies a succession of interpretations.

Painting only acquires value when it offers itself as definitive, when it constitutes its own world, its own ambition, its own projection, not closely restricted to aesthetic observations. Everything relating to technique, for instance, is strictly between the painter and himself. To the amateur, the viewer, the painting presents itself as a completed object. How it was arrived at is something that no one, barring the specialist, need ever know.

In their definitive state, the drawing, the sheet of paper, the canvas propose a contact with the reality of everyday life, or a reconstructed reality, or surreality, or the entire range of all parallels to reality.

Whichever the case, it must be understood that painting—except where it limits itself to decorative effects, which is the antithesis of the principle of art—is essentially information on the mental universe of the painter.

As in all artistic disciplines, what does not emerge from a strong internal life, which is to say an acute sense of the real, is devoid of significance and is unfailingly erased by time. A work of art is not execution. A work of art is revelation.

Found again in Rilke
the idea of our faces
forming a succession in time. . . .
The question arises of
knowing what happens
to our past likenesses,
these vague milestones,
these fleeting shadows
in a continuous sequence
that no memory other than
a technological one can retain.
This remark also brings out
the transformative function
of chronology.

—Louis Calaferte, *Le Spectateur immobile,*
Carnets IV, 1978–1979

. . . .

Louis Calaferte. Blaisy-Bas, 1992. (Photograph, Louis Monier)

chronology

1928

On July 14, Louis Calaferte born in Turin, Italy. Childhood in the slums of Lyons.

1941

During the German occupation, at the age of thirteen, begins to work in a factory, then in a workshop.

1946

Together with a friend, arrives in Paris utterly destitute, intending to become an actor. Takes walk-on roles at the Théâtre du Vieux-Colombier and the Théâtre de l'Odéon. Works as a film extra. As a student actor, prepares Racine's *Britannicus* with Jean Davy.

1947–48

Lives at 9 rue Greffulhe, the Hotel Mary. Writes for the theater, with encouragement from the actor Guy Rapp. Begins thousand-page book, "La Charogne" [Carrion], never completed.

1949–50

Writes *Requiem des innocents.*

1952

Sponsored by Joseph Kessel, *Requiem des innocents* published by Editions René Julliard.

1953

Despite immediate success of first book, Louis Calaferte leaves Paris and returns to Lyons.

1956

Settles in Mornant, on the outskirts of Lyons. On November 5 begins writing *Septentrion.*

1957

Becomes producer and host of a radio show on literature and drama for Radio-Lyon.

1962

On August 16, finishes writing *Septentrion.*

1963

Septentrion published in a private edition, through the Cercle Précieux du Livre, Claude Tchou. Book immediately banned from publication by the Ministry of the Interior. Publication of a collection of stories, *No Man's Land,* by Editions Julliard.

1968

Satori and *Rosa Mystica* published by Editions Denoël.

1973

Calaferte leaves job as a radio producer and decides to make living by writing. His first play, *Chez les Titch,* produced at the Petit Odéon, directed by Jean-Pierre Miquel.

1978

Ibsen Prize for his play *Les Miettes* at the Théâtre Essaïon.

1980

Publication of first volume of his *Carnets* [*Notebooks*],
Le Chemin de Sion.

1983

Prix de l'Académie française for *Ebauche d'un autoportrait.*

1984

First real publication of *Septentrion* since its banning in 1963.
Calaferte awarded the Grand Prix de la Ville de Paris for the
body of his plays.

1992

Awarded the Grand Prix National des Lettres.

1993

His play *Opéra bleu* produced at the Théâtre du Lucernaire,
directed by Victor Viala and Sylvie Favre. Calaferte named a
chevalier of the National Order of Merit.

1994

On May 2, Calaferte dies.

notes

Preface

1. Louis Calaferte, *Le Chemin de Sion* (Paris: Denoël, 1980), 141.

2. Louis Calaferte, *L'Or et le Plomb* (Paris: Denoël, 1981), 115.

3. Calaferte, *Le Chemin de Sion,* 319.

4. Louis Calaferte, *Le Spectateur immobile* (Paris: L'Arpenteur-Gallimard, 1990), 24.

5. Søren Kierkegaard, *For Self-Examination; Judge for Yourself!* edited and translated by Howard V. Hong and Edna H. Hong (Princeton, N.J.: Princeton University Press, 1990).

6. Calaferte, *Le Chemin de Sion,* 216.

7. Calaferte, *L'Or et le Plomb,* 151.

The Dark Forces

1. "But thou, when thou prayest, enter into thy closet, and when thou hast shut thy door, pray to thy Father which is in secret; and thy Father which seeth in secret shall reward thee openly." Matt. 6:6.

2. Georges Bataille, *L'Erotisme* (Paris: Editions de Minuit, 1985), 136.

3. Stephen Hawking, *A Brief History of Time* (New York: Bantam, 1988), 122, 106.

4. *C. G. Jung parle* (Editions Buchet-Chastel, 1989), 180.

5. Henry Miller, *The Time of the Assassins: A Study of Rimbaud* (Norfolk, Conn.: New Directions, 1956), 36.

Of Spiritual Factors

1. Eugen Drewermann, *La Parole qui guérit* (Editions du Cerf, 1991), 67.

The Way It Works with Women

1. Georges Bataille, *L'Erotisme* (Paris: Editions de Minuit, 1985), 161.

2. "In my own world, there is no room for anti-Semitism or racial prejudice of any kind. I want men to be free, emancipated, unfettered by bigotry or prejudice, fear or anxiety." From a letter written by Henry Miller to Maurice Girodias. Published in William Blake, ed., *Cahiers Henry Miller,* 1 (Bordeaux: 1994).

The Sands of Time

1. Louis-Ferdinand Céline, *L'Ecole des cadavres* (Paris: Editions Denoël, 1938), 284.

2. Céline, *Bagatelles pour un massacre* (Paris: Editions Denoël, 1937), 317, 319.

3. "Today Dreyfus seems to me completely harmless. Either he has received repeated sunstroke or he is progressing toward general paralysis. . . . He lacks all intelligence, he has been serinated." Maurice Barrès, *Mes Cahiers* (Editions Plon, 1930), vol. 2, page 143, 1898–1902.

An Island of Resistance

1. The film resulting from this collaboration, directed by Jean-

Pierre Pauty and with the painter René Strubel, is titled
An Island of Resistance. Its running time is fifty-two minutes.
Music: Pascal Mikaélian. Camera: Benoît Rizzotti. Second
Camera: Claude Guéguan. Editor: Catherine Dehaut. Key
Light Productions, Paris, 1994.

Intimist Theater and Baroque Theater

Gathered here are Louis Calaferte's comments on the two facets
of his theater writing, recorded at the Petit Odéon Theater during the filming of *Un îlot de résistance.* Louis Calaferte's complete
plays have been published in three volumes: *Pièces intimistes* (Ed.
Hesse: Blois, 1993) and *Pièces baroques* (two vols., Ed. Hesse:
Blois, 1994).

Painting

This text was originally intended as a voice-over to accompany
the sequence in the film *Un îlot de résistance* dealing with Louis
Calaferte's painting. It could not be preserved in the final cut.

Louis Calaferte. Lyons, 1974. (Photograph, collection G. Calaferte)

bibliography

Narratives

Requiem des innocents. Paris: Julliard, 1952. Reprinted Collection 10/18, 1980.

Partage des vivants. Paris: Julliard, 1953.

Septentrion. Tchou, 1963. Reprinted Denoël, Collection Folio, 1990.

No Man's Land. Paris: Julliard, 1963.

Rosa mystica. Paris: Denoël, 1968.

Satori. Paris: Denoël, 1968.

Portrait de l'enfant. Paris: Denoël, 1969.

Hinterland. Paris: Denoël, 1971.

Limitrophe. Paris: Denoël, 1972.

La Vie parallèle. Paris: Denoël, 1974.

Episodes de la vie des mantes religieuses. Paris: Denoël, 1976.

Campagnes. Paris: Denoël, 1979.

Ebauche d'un autoportrait. Paris: Denoël, 1983.

L'Incarnation. Paris: Denoël, 1987.

Promenade dans un parc: Récits. Paris: Denoël, 1987.

Memento mori. Paris: L'Arpenteur-Gallimard, 1988.

La Mécanique des femmes. Paris: L'Arpenteur-Gallimard, 1992. Published in English as *The Way It Works with Women,* translated by Sarah Harrison (Evanston, Ill.: Marlboro Press/Northwestern University Press, 1998).

C'est la guerre. Paris: L'Arpenteur-Gallimard, 1993. Published in English as *C'est la Guerre,* translated by Austryn Wainhouse (Evanston, Ill.: Marlboro Press/Northwestern University Press, 1999).

Essays

Les Sables du temps. Paris: Le Tout sur le Tout, 1988.

Droit de cité. Levallois-Perret: Manya, 1992.

Notebooks and Interviews

Le Chemin de Sion: Carnets 1956–1967. Paris: Denoël, 1980.

L'Or et le Plomb: Carnets 1968–1973. Paris: Denoël, 1981.

Lignes intérieures: Carnets 1974–1977. Paris: Denoël, 1985.

Une vie, une déflagration: Entretiens avec Louis Calaferte. Interviews and introduction by Patrick Amine. Paris: Denoël, 1985.

Le Spectateur immobile: Carnets 1978–1979. Paris: L'Arpenteur-Gallimard, 1990.

Miroir de Janus: Carnets 1980–1981. Paris: L'Arpenteur-Gallimard, 1993.

Rapports: Carnets 1982. Paris: Gallimard, 1996.

Choses dites: Entretiens et choix de textes. Eds. Guillemette Calaferte, Ingrid Naour, Pierre Drachline. Paris: Le Cherche midi, 1997.

Plays

Mégaphonie. Paris: Stock, 1972.

Chez les Titch and *Trafic*. L'Avant-Scène. 1975.

Les Mandibules and Mo. Paris: Stock, 1976.

L'Amour des mots and *Revue du CDN de Reims*, 2. 1979.

Théâtre intimiste (Chez les Titch, Trafic, Les Miettes, Tu as bien fais de venir, Paul). Paris: Stock, 1980.

Les Derniers Devoirs. Revue du CDN de Reims, 16. *L'Avant-Scène*. 1983.

Aux armes citoyens!: Baroquerie en un acte avec couplets. Paris: Denoël, 1986.

Théâtre complet: Pièces Intimistes (1 volume) and *Pièces Baroques* (2 volumes). Blois: Ed. Hesse, 1993–94.

Poetry

Rag-Time. Paris: Denoël, 1972.

Paraphe. Paris: Denoël, 1974.

Londonniennes. Paris: Le Tout sur le Tout, 1985.

ABCD, enfantines. With illustrations by Jacques Truphémus. Lausanne: Editions Bellefontaine, 1987.

Décalcomanies. With lithographs by Pierre Ardouvin. Editions Grande Nature, 1987.

Nuit close. Paris: Editions Fourbis, 1988.

Télégrammes de nuit. With lithographs by Catherine Seghers. Blois: Editions Tarabuste et La Marge, 1988.

Danse découpage. With illustrations by Philippe Cognée. Saint-Benoît-du-Sault: Editions Tarabuste, 1989.

Faire-part: 20 poèmes élastiques. With illustrations by the author. Paris: Editions Deyrolle, 1991.

Haïkaï du jardin. Paris: L'Arpenteur-Gallimard, 1991.

Silex (originally published in *Rag-Time*). With illustrations by Jacques Truphémus. Lyons: Les Sillons du Temps, 1991.

Fruits. With illustrations by the author. Saint-Claude-de-Diray, France: Ed. Hesse, 1992.

Les Métamorphoses du revolver. In *Triages*, 3 (1992). Subsequently published as a book with illustrations by Franck Na (Saint-Montan, 1993).

L'Arbre à sanglots. With an engraving by the author. Ivry-sur-Seine: Les Ateliers d'Art Vincent Rougier, 1993.

Nativité. With illustrations by Lise-Marie Brochen, Christine Crozat, Claire Lesteven, Frédérique Lucien, Kate Van Houten, and Marie-Laure Viale. Saint-Benoît-du-Sault: Editions Tarabuste, 1994.

Ton nom est sexe. With illustrations by Denis Poupeville. Editions les Autodidactes, 1994.

L'Homme vivant. Paris: Gallimard, 1994.

Art-signal: Expressions poétiques. Saint-Claude-de-Diray, France: Ed. Hesse, 1996.

Films

Les Territoires de Louis Calaferte. A film by Michel Van Zèle, 1988.

Un îlot de résistance. A film by Jean-Pierre Pauty, 1993.

Radio

Interviews with Pierre Drachline, "A voix nue." France-Culture, 1986.

Exhibitions

Galerie Corine Martin. Miribel-Lyon, 1973. Drawings.

Théâtre Essaïon. Paris, 1986. Collages.

Bibliothèque municipale de Lyon Part-Dieu. Lyons, 1988. Drawings, collages, objects, installations.

Librairie Biffure. Paris, 1988. Drawings, collages.

Librairie L'Arbre à Lettres. Paris, 1991. Drawings, objects.

Librairie L'Arbre à Lettres. Paris, 1992, 1993. Drawings.

Galerie La Marge. Blois, 1992, 1993. Drawings.
Centre Culturel de Saint-Benoît-du-Sault. Saint-Benoît-du-
    Sault, 1992. Drawings, collages, objects.
Château de Talcy, 1993. Drawings.
Librairie Ombres Blanches. Toulouse, 1993. Drawings.

Louis Calaferte was born in Turin in 1928. He was a playwright, poet, and writer of prose. His other works include *C'est la Guerre* and *The Way It Works with Women,* both published by the Marlboro Press/Northwestern. He died in 1994.

Jean-Pierre Pauty is a director whose works include the 1993 documentary on Louis Calaferte entitled *Un îlot de résistance.*